CLINCH *the* DEAL

Negotiation Strategies to Get What You Want

CLINCH *the* DEAL

Negotiation Strategies to Get What You Want

Manuj Desai

Indus Source Books

Indian Spirit, Universal Wisdom

Indus Source Books
PO Box 6194
Malabar Hill PO
Mumbai 400 006
INDIA
Email: info@indussource.com
www.indussource.com

Clinch the Deal: Negotiation Strategies to Get What You Want

First published in India by Indus Source Books in 2017

ISBN: 978-93-85509-06-3

Cover design by Sanskruti Graphics, Mumbai

Printed at Thomson Press India Ltd., New Delhi.

Contents

This book is dedicated to my father, Shri Tapasvi Desai, a mathematician who has influenced and shaped the life of his students including myself, coaching us on invaluable lessons of life.

Acknowledgements

This book would not have been in the shape it is today if it were not for:

My parents, family, wide array of friends, acquaintances, and "others" who knowingly or unknowingly contributed to the thought which eventually shaped into this book.

Finhas Merchant, my guardian angel, whose fond memories I cherish every day.

My special thanks to my publisher Sonavi Desai and her team at Indus Source Books.

Chapter 1

Introduction

The world is becoming a smart place, and we are living completely under the influence of technology; what has not changed and probably will not change are the characteristics of humans. Humans tend to remain in their comfort zone, and as soon as they are exposed to things outside their comfort zone, they struggle.

Negotiation is an essential element of every person's life, whether in the professional or personal area. I looked at the existing set of books available on negotiation skills for understanding their content and found that most books just focus on how to negotiate, merely offering techniques; the identification of the core of the subject was not well-articulated in the other materials I read and searched. This book focuses on understanding the agenda of the individuals which, if done right, can help set the tone for what could be achieved out of a discussion.

The human brain has a funny composition, while it remembers a lot, it forgets a lot too.

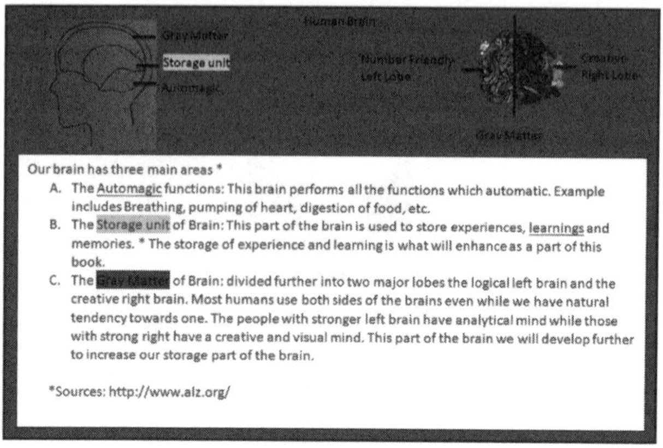

Figure 1

As humans, at times we know our limits and potential, while there are some unexplored territories where we don't look at our own potential and cave in even before we start. My first chapter is all about that feeling. **You cannot succeed in anything if your brain is not in the right place.** The book focuses on building your inner strength, while giving you resources and tools that help you change what you don't want to accept. There are techniques in the book that help build your tolerance, needed for you to tackle things that you don't have power over but which you still want to influence. The book will help you tackle the "unknown" territories in a situation where the outcome will be one that will make you smile. There are a few facts that should be highlighted before we get too deep into the book. No one knows your situation better than you do. You know what you know, **you have learned from your own upbringing** and what you have seen of the world. For anyone to come and advise you would be wrong since they cannot bring themselves into the same circumstances and the state of mind you are in. All said and done **you remain the perfect judge for your situation.** One can try to learn from others' learnings or mistakes and take corrective actions. There is a term called "Intention", which remains the fulcrum of any discussion. Not sure if you have heard this before, **"you are who you are, and will remain who you are".** Every individual is different. There can be similarities in some areas of your lives or some choices of two individuals might be similar but that doesn't detract from you being the "one you are". The other fact remains—never compare yourself with others. There will be people who will have better or lesser skills than you are, hence comparing yourself with others will lead to unnecessary grief or ego boost. Focus on what you can do right, focus on winning in every situation specially getting your message across correctly, and never focus on defeating the other individual. Negotiation can extend from simple to tough situations, can damage relationships if not done right, can make unnecessary noise that could be more than what you can or would want to handle. The key is to have the right tools which can help you "skillfully navigate" the known and unknown territories.

Let me illustrate a situation to you. We were on a family trip visiting a hill station called "Mandu" in the central India. The region being notorious as a "not so safe" area, especially in the late evening, we wanted to get to the final destination before dark. As expected we were running late due to multiple issues with the vehicle we were travelling in. It was a rented van which could accommodate 18 passengers. As the early hours of the evening approached, we were stopped by the local police and it was recommended that the road ahead was not safe and to get to our destination we would have to take a detour, which was a longer route. Our quick research indicated that the detour was the right thing to do and we took the detour. Now the concern was not only security but also time and fatigue as the travel time was getting longer. We had kids with us as well; entertaining them through the journey was a different challenge. Our enthusiasm was still high and with the right zeal we eventually made it to the foothills of the hill station to find out that the road uphill was closed by the security appointed by the local tourism in charge. They had manual road block to control the traffic entry to the place. The entire situation took a wrong turn when the guards refused to open the gates as based on their stand operating procedure (SOP) they were not supposed to open the gates beyond a particular time. We asked for the SOP and there was none available with them. We made a few phone calls, the guards made a few phone calls. Everyone was losing patience and the kids were getting cranky. The distance from the foothills to the hotel was 16 KM (10 miles), which, in normal conditions, would have taken us about 30 minutes. After waiting for an hour at the entry point, we were really losing patience. One of my relatives took a stone and tried to break the lock of the manual gate. That moment was a trigger for the guards to take action before the situation got desperate.

The end goal for us was to reach the hotel. Finally, we took control of the situation, had the guards open the gates and we did reach the hotel. But at one point it really seemed as though that discussion could have gone haywire if we had not taken control of the situation.

One clear understanding that I have had through my experience is **"life is not fair – start getting used to it"**. This, I believe, is a moment where we sink or swim. We need to try our potential every minute. People like us, the normal human beings, need to negotiate every day, every minute.

All our life we have negotiated, believe it or not.

As kids we negotiated with our parents,

At school and college we negotiated with our colleagues and teachers,

At work we negotiated with our seniors and juniors,

In business we negotiate with our clients,

In a later part of our life we negotiate with our kids or our grand kids

And we negotiate with our spouse or partner all the time.

This fact never changes—we negotiate more often than we think we negotiate. These days I see myself negotiating heavily with my kids; it reminds me of my days as a kid negotiating with my parents. While I feel that my kids are smarter than I was at the same age, today I have to fry my brain trying to keep up with their smartness. Sometimes we also negotiate with the almighty :).

At times, we end up negotiating with ourselves. It would not be a completely true statement, that to negotiate you need two or more entities; when we negotiate with our self, we have two thoughts which have potentially different endings. Fluctuating mind or non-decisive mind causes more pain since you are controlled by multiple thoughts and when you cannot reach a consensus you end up with wrong choices or choices that you never wanted in the first place.

This brings up a great perspective "keeping the end in mind". Every negotiation starts with a reason and would end somewhere. While we would always wish that the end would be in our favour, does that happen every time? This book talks about real life techniques and helps articulate real life scenarios. Some chapters focus solely on individual personalities and techniques to deal with those personalities.

All situations, no matter how different they are, have three things in common:

1. Need to get into the particular situation (in other terms, WHY).
2. A starting point where the situation begins (in other terms, HOW).
3. And an end (in other terms, what one achieved), where eventually the negotiation will end.

One additional lesson I have learned is to keep in mind that all battles are not worth fighting for, so pick your battles carefully. Picking your battles carefully takes us into the next topic of identifying your need. A simple message I have learned in life is "people will be people" and you will meet all types of people who will challenge your potential. **You will have to deal with people outside your comfort zone, whether you like it or not.** So there is no harm in being prepared for what is definitely going to come your way....

"Since life should be simple - don't complicate things unnecessarily", is the other message articulated in the book.

Throughout this book we will improve our gray matter and hence enhance our storage units.

The Book is organized in 6 sections or steps. Figure 2 below indicates the flow of the steps. Each step is crucial in the process to reach the stage of negotiation where the techniques help with the actual negotiation. The chapters in the book eventually map back to one of the 6 steps as depicted in Figure 3. Steps 1 to 6 should be followed to achieve the "Need". How one applies the learnings is based on their grasp of the chapters articulated in the book. My recommendation would be to go through the book just like a novel the first time as some of the chapters in the later part of the book also help with formalizing the thought processes.

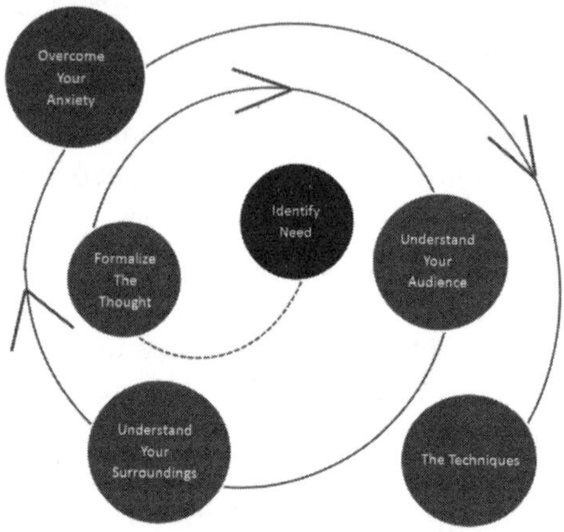

Figure 2

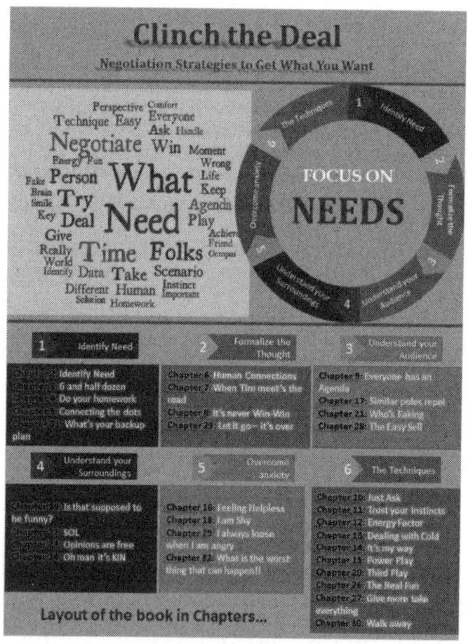

Figure 3

The myth of negotiation mostly gets interpreted as "confrontation" or "conflict resolution". The idea of the book is to understand the myth and separate "understanding agenda", "actual negotiation", and terms like "conflict resolution" and help put them under the real perspective lens of "need" and methods to achieve the "need".

I am going to talk about two terms which are used in the human psychology study a lot; it's called WIIFM meaning (What's In It For Me) and WIIFY meaning (What's In It For You)

WIIFM? vs *WIIFY?*

This book focuses on understanding the agenda so one can then focus on the "What's In It For You vs What's In It For Me". The actual negotiation is really a simple process; we humans make it complicated as we have not spent time to understand the agenda and continue down a never ending path as we are not clear on either our need or the need of the person we are dealing with.

According to the articles written on the web*, actual negotiation has been categorized into 5 simple styles:

1. **Accommodating:** People who focus on preserving relationship and are always eager to help solve other person's problems.
2. **Avoiding:** People who just do not like to negotiate. They "Avoid" and dodge the confrontational aspects of negotiation.
3. **Collaborating:** People who enjoy negotiation and include others in the decision process.
4. **Competing:** People who just want to win an argument.
5. **Compromising:** People who are eager to just close the discussion, they are also called the give some take some negotiations.

(*Source: https://en.wikipedia.org/wiki/Negotiation)

While these are already known facts and are commonly used in the society today, the lack of material on understanding the Agenda of the people involved with us in our day to day discussion is the root of this book. The process of negotiation and the time to negotiate can sometimes drain people out and in the end people end up caving into the discussion or rather giving up the discussion even without trying it. If your needs are clear and if you have the power to understand the "Exact" need of the person you are going to be dealing with it will reduce the "stress", "tension", "time", and solely focus on "Why" a person is doing what he is doing.

Chapter 2

Identify Your Needs

Before getting into negotiating your needs you should be clear in your mind. A study on choices indicates that the less number of choices humans have, the faster we get to decisions. Our needs could be high or low based on the situation we are in. One might reach a point when the particular need becomes low. Those are battles you want to think through whether to pursue. (Read a later chapter of this book "Let it go—it's over".) Here is my recommendation:

If it interests you a bit then it's worth trying for.

So even if the need is low or very low, what do you have to lose to give it a try? If there is no need, you will not even think about the situation or the thing. Make a note of the need you have, put everything on the paper. Remember there could be need of the hour which could be different from the need of the month to need of the year. Put that on the paper; in the later chapters we will figure out how to prioritize and achieve those needs. Each one of us is unique and so are our needs. Don't try to boil the entire ocean in one go. Keep it under 5 and then prioritize them in the order of highest to lowest. There are times when we run into scenarios where we have no clue if we have a need or not. This is ok. After all we are human beings and yes we get confused easily. The other fact is at every stage in life the need is different so we need to prioritize. At any given point in time there can be more than one need.

For our situation of need let's consider this example:

You are walking in a supermarket. You have nothing to buy or no agenda or no list that you are tracking. You have enough money to buy the entire supermarket so you do not have to worry about what you pick and what you don't. What will you do?

- When I ask this question to a bunch of college kids they give me a look that says, "Why would I go to a store when I don't need anything, and these days we have online applications for groceries so why go to a store in the first place?"
- The same question if asked to a bunch of grown-ups would elicit a response such as, "Oh, we will buy everything in the supermarket." Of course, they have no idea where they will store it.
- From an entrepreneur I would get a reply such as, "If I have enough money I will just own the entire supermarket."

Needs are different hence the difference in the answer.

This highlights a key characteristic of humans: Sometimes we are really sure what our needs are and sometimes we have no clue. Before you get into any type of negotiating see if you can identify your need clearly in your mind. We will address the point about how we can articulate our need in the later chapters. It is the need that drives us all. I have had people come up to me and say: Your chapter "Identify Your Need" talks about how everyone has a need but what if we don't have any need? My basic question to them is: Do you mean you have no need in a particular situation or you don't have any need whatsoever? If the reply is: "Oh I don't have any need at all" my response remains "You should have attained Nirvana by now, help me attain it too!" What should be clear in mind is, we have needs and that it is essential to sort out the priorities in mind. That is where some of the techniques in this book will help articulate what the actual need is. So let's sort out first things first. Find your need. Craving could be other term for the need. So this chapter can also be termed as **"find your cravings"**. What do you want from every scenario that you are faced with? Some people have a habit of "going with the flow" where they have no need, no craving and no preference. Now, that would be a scary moment. No matter how basic the need or craving is, you need to be clear what it is. To the dispassionate, the need might just be having peace of mind or calmness within you. That still is a need. The way I see it is, we humans will be continuing on the path to satisfy our needs, hence the key is to get it right the first time. Some people are really focused while others are on the "easy to go" path. My recommendation is:

Take time, think of what you need.

The seemingly obvious might not be what you would be chasing in the first place. As called out earlier, the need of the hour could be different from the need of the day, the need of the month could be different than the need of the year. It all depends on the stage you are in. As kids, I wish someone would have told us "clearly" to get our needs straight, be it in sports, in education, or in areas like entrepreneurship. If the need is clear then one must work on setting up the right environment to achieve that need. Wait!! Did you think that by identifying your need accurately you are done? Oh no! This is where we start. This is where almost everything starts. I am not asking people to be visionaries just yet. If you can be or are one, then the path to achieve it would be easy. Common people like us have to first identify the need, figure out the path to achieve the need, set the vision to achieve the need and take baby steps to reach it.

Why baby steps? One cannot chew food easily with a mouth full, baby steps or little bites will help you reach the need faster and will give you enough time to course-correct if you fail.

Why am I talking about failure here in the first chapter? Since that remains the fact. If we go by experience then the chances of failure will reduce. Just think of any recent accident that you were involved in. Did you plan it? No. No one loves accidents, but they happen, so what do you do? Learn from that accident and plan not to do it again. This, in human terms, is called experience. Knowing the "impact" is what I like to call it. People that know me or have worked with me before know this statement by heart now. This is one of my favourite ones on "articulation of impact". "If you come and tell me there is a car in the middle of the road, it does not mean anything to me. But if you come and tell me that there is a car in the middle of the road and if I don't slow down I will meet with an accident, you have articulated the 'impact' to me." And we humans have a better tendency to react if we know the "impact". All I am trying to do here is to highlight the "impact" of "need". The sooner one realizes the need, the better it is because one can start planning for the same. It is good to know what you are looking for or "fighting for". There are people, who, after years don't know their need. Just one piece of advice here—you have a need and now is a time to think about it, before it is really late. There have been times when I have had to ask myself what drives me, whether I have everything I need to motivate me and keep me functional. We get so involved with the situations that we forget there is life beyond that situation as well. I often use this statement:

Don't get caught in the situation.

It's ok. "Life is not fair – get used to it".

Now that you have a solid idea about the need you have, let's get through some techniques which will help you to get your needs prioritized right. Keep your list ready.

If your list seems to be getting bigger than 5, Great!!! However, prioritize which are the top 5. After you achieve the first top 5 needs, look at the next 5. Do not try to achieve everything at one time. Remember: "Baby Steps" not "Laundry list". The need is to be added to the "storage unit of the brain". (Fig. 1)

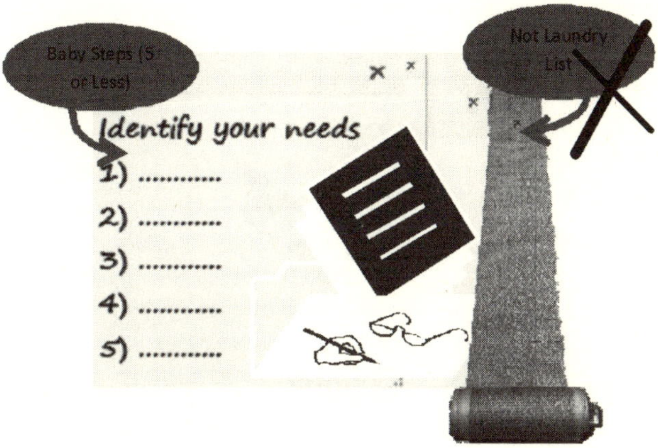

Figure 4

Key Learnings

1. Identify your need.

2. Chart out the path to achieve it.

3. Take baby steps towards it.

Chapter 3

Six and Half-Dozen

Six of one and half a dozen of the other, is a well-known idiom. Since dozen means 12; what is half a dozen? In numbers it means six (6). The point here is they both mean the same but it's the perspective: one can say six or one can say half-dozen. This chapter helps with the articulation of the need.

You want to get into negotiation because you care.

"It's all a matter of mind, if you don't mind it does not matter." This famous saying is applicable here. Because you care about the situation you feel like understanding the agenda to help with negotiating or in other terms you should try to understand the agenda first if you care. This chapter focuses on the idea of need and how to explore your need and that of the other person. It took me a while to get to where I am. The world was not built in a day and while we all understand it takes patience and perseverance to achieve good results we end up losing to the sheer urgency to reach the finish line. Technically, there is no finish line. As soon as you reach one there is another one, which you will see at a distance. The key point of this chapter is to make one realize that just as we care about something, the people we are dealing with care about something as well.

About three years ago, I saw a small puppy playing by the side of the road. I turned my face to the traffic on the road and before I realized, the puppy yelped. A bus had gone over it! All I could hear was a cry. Not knowing exactly what had happened, in panic I tried to get the puppy to a safe place. The puppy did not let me come close, maybe it was scared or in pain. At that time, I was the only one trying to help the puppy. Seeing me, a few more people came to help. We lifted the puppy and took it to safety. Two days later when I saw the puppy running around again, it made me feel good. I felt that I had helped. The reason for adding this incident to the chapter is to highlight that as human beings we care; we might not show it often but we really do care.

Another example that comes to mind is how we deal with our kids. We all try to coach our kids when we feel they are doing something wrong or appreciate them when they do something right. We do this because we care.

The six and half-dozen analogy fits into the idea of care. We have a tendency called "it's ok". This is all I could do or in other words why should I try so hard, I have what I have. But why shouldn't you try? After all you have nothing to lose.

We are human beings and yes, we care. At times showing the care also helps to empathize with the individuals we are dealing with. In reality what I have seen is no matter how hard you are trying to win the entire gamut of whatever you are trying to negotiate, the human factor in you is stopping you from pushing that limit beyond a certain point. People ask me if there is a difference in the way people try to negotiate based on gender, race, or age factors. While there is enough research done on these topics already, in my experience, having seen people from all genders, multiple races and age groups, the **Need** and **Agenda** fall in line with each other. The focus on the need and the agenda have not been called out this explicitly in the past. There is certainly, based on the age and maturity of the individual, difference in the "need" and the zeal to achieve the need. Does this mean that adults have a good handle on understanding the agenda? Not really. In fact, the research by US National Library of Medicine and National Institute of Health indicates that adolescence is the best age for starting to make good judgements on understanding the agenda. However, the challenge with this age is that sometimes the maturity level limits the ability to understand the "exact" agenda as the idea of looking at the larger picture mostly does not exist.

Women are said to be more compassionate then men; however, this cannot be generalized. Again it depends on the maturity of the person, the amount of grey matter and the way the storage unit is structured. The same is with age and race. The ability to understand the agenda depends more on individuals and the type of individuals they are rather than gender, race, and age factors. These factors play a role to some extent but one cannot make decisions merely based on these factors. There was a reason I added these factors here in the topic six and half-dozen. The fact that I am trying to highlight here is all depends on the "need" and the perspective of the individual you end up dealing with. Understanding "why" a person is doing something is more relevant than "what" the person is doing. The ideal scenario is looking at the problem statement and spending more time on understanding the true problem than providing solutions by jumping to conclusions without exactly understanding the problem statement. As we always say, solutions are easy if we know what the "exact" problem is.

According to research*, the mirror neuron present in the brain helps one perform a similar act to what one sees someone else perform. This research, however, is based on the study of animals; the study of mirror neurons in humans is still based on a lot of guesswork. One of the conclusions which researchers have inferred is that the mirror neurons may be critical to understanding how one behaves and the actions one takes.

For our discussion the message is crucial. "Need" is what

---

*Source: https://en.wikipedia.org/wiki/Mirror_neuron

drives us as humans and if we can understand "why" someone behaves in a particular manner, our job to understand the agenda becomes easy. You will remain who you are, you can learn or unlearn based on the environment you are exposed to, and this is what we call "ability", which improves with practice and understanding. In other terms, we also call this the maturity of a human being or richness of the grey matter. If we already have been through a similar situation then we can dip into our storage unit to look for pre-existing solutions, else the grey matter has to think of solutions and then enrich and update our storage unit for future use.

Now look at the first item on the list we created in Chapter 2. The highest need should be prioritized as number 1 and the lowest as number 5.

Key Learnings

---

1. Identify the need of the other person.

2. Understand why he is doing what he is doing.

Chapter 4

Do Your Homework

In the earlier chapters we talked about us, the normal human beings, who at times are confused, or have a "six and half-dozen" mind. From this chapter onwards we start to focus on getting your inner self trained to understand the agenda of others.

This is your "inner Octopus" that you want tamed; to handle every scenario in life.

The Octopus, considered a metaphor for change or tuning in the book, is a very powerful but a spineless animal. Octopuses can navigate through very small places, have special pigments in the skin that helps them with camouflaging, have great problem-solving skills, can squirt out ink to confuse their predators, can multitask, and their flexible body allows them to camouflage themselves as their predators. Understanding the agenda is mostly based on a situation as one reacts based on the situation they are in and as always one size does not fit all. The basic step is to do your homework and do it right. There will always be scenarios when you are not prepared; we will talk about those scenarios in later chapters like SOL and Dealing with Cold. For now, let's get to the basics: if the need is high, do your homework right, and when I say do your homework I mean it. These days there are so many options available to do your homework. When I was a school student the only resource I had was called MOM. We also had libraries, teachers and DAD but who would bother with those? MOM somehow had all the answers. If she didn't, it was her problem to find them! Now the internet is a great resource to do the homework. But there is a catch here: If you just do your homework on the internet then that technique is available to all, hence what would be your "unique selling point" also widely referred as USP? I have seen the local newspapers bring in great perspective and they should be considered a tool to do homework as well. The next one would be advertisements. A common reaction to this is: Now I have to look at advertisements too? Seriously? What you are looking for is called "Clue". Yes, the same clue one that is so vital in detective stories. You want to know the pulse and have your clues lined up. People on the science side of human behaviour call it "Databit", which helps to provide information that is needed to make necessary decisions. This is where we get serious. Keep your eyes and ears open, collect as much data as you can. Getting the events in sequence will help you stay focused. Collecting data and getting the data right will really help you to be honest with yourself and prove yourself right. Just gathering the data will not help, you will have to connect your data together to make a story from the same. Constantly processing data, organizing the data and connecting them together will give you the necessary nudge that you will need for understanding the agenda. I will repeat this statement at multiple levels in this book: ***You negotiate when the need is high,*** and if the need is high then it becomes absolutely critical to get your "ducks in a row".

I had a friend trying to change her job to a different country due to family reasons; she wanted to be closer to her immediate family. The first thing I heard from her was that there were no jobs like the ones she was looking for, in that particular country. I sat with her to identify her need and yes, it was high. So we looked at places where she was looking to get her data, found out that multiple websites that had job postings had been overlooked. That was missing in her method. Nothing is easy but when the need is high you prioritize accordingly.

When I hear: "I looked but could not find it" or "I could not find the 'clue'" I ask the next question: "Did you look in all places and did you look hard enough?" It's all there as needed, you just have to find it. Did you watch for any "micro-inequity" or "micro-messaging" in the discussions, may be that is what you missed. In a nut-shell "micro-messaging" stands for unconscious messages which people pass all the time; it's a signal that you do not want to miss as they just gave out their entire "agenda" through a micro-message. There are multiple micro-messages that pass through a discussion, which, if observed correctly, can change the entire discussion. Obviously one will not learn to recognize these easily. It takes practice, and a very thorough observation to master these techniques.

I was once having a discussion with one of my team members. The discussion went off on a tangent when he expressed concern about being unable to understand the intent of the person he talked with. I rolled up my sleeves and asked him, "Do you know what this action of mine means?" He stared at me with a blank face. I ended up explaining my journey of how I started to observe and the challenges I personally faced while trying to understand the micro-messages.

Me: When I rolled up my sleeves, my action meant that it's a topic of my interest and that I am passionate about the same. It also meant, let's talk.

Team member: Body language is much more meaningful, I guess.

Me: Yes it is, more than what you can imagine, but observing the body movements and verbally listening to the discussion are two separate activities which require practice to implement.

Team member: How did you start to observe, did you have challenges?

Me: Oh Yes!! Initially, while it intrigued me a lot, it was difficult for me to observe the actions and listen to the topic of discussion as well. I remember the first time I tried this, I failed miserably.

Team member (looking puzzled): Really?

Me: Yes, in my first observation session, I kept looking straight at the person I was talking to. As soon as the individual would look in any other direction, I was, in my mind jumping to conclusions; "he looked left" – he must be recollecting something from his memory, wait! He raised his eyebrows, wait! he moved his head......and this observation went on.

Team member: So that's good, right? You were able to observe most of the signs.

Me: Kind of, but I could not pay attention to the topic of discussion, I just kept observing him. This meant, I tried to understand his intent but had no clue about the topic as I could not listen to the discussion properly. So at the end of the discussion, I was clueless about it.

Team member: So how did you pick up observing and listening at the same time?

Me: I told myself, next time I have a one-on-one with someone, I won't focus on any other technique. Just look at the eyes and see if the person looks left or right obviously along with trying to listen as well. I decided that I will have to be well composed, prepared and keep a distraction to slow the discussion which will give me time to catch up if I lose the track of observing or listening. The distraction should not look out of place and should deliberately stop the discussion just for a few seconds, so I could use my grey matter to analyze and think. I kept a bottle of water with me, thinking it will keep me hydrated, my mind oxygenated and also act as the distraction method I was looking for.

Team Member: So did that work? It was only looking to the left and right? Or did that include noticing the head as well?

Me: There are meanings to the head movement. However, I had decided that I would not try too many things at once as I start my journey, just focus on the eyes. Looking left is analyzing the situation or trying to remember a real instance. Looking right is mostly fabricating. Left could also mean thinking hard to remember what happened or what might have happened.

Team member: Aah! So you took the baby steps you keep on talking about? And slowly added one more technique after you got a handle on the eye movement.

Me: Bingo! Try it next time. You have a one-on-one with your team member and let me know the output of that discussion. If it does not get you the results the first time, don't worry. Keep trying. It takes a little while but you will get there.

Now, let us cover a few of the micro-messages in the table below and then through the book. As needed, I will highlight a few more that are relevant to the scenarios. Try adding these to the storage unit of your brain.

Micro-message	**Implied meaning**
Unnecessary wink	Trying to act friendly or act of superiority
Looking at the watch multiple times when talking	Trying to show, the person is in a rush and needs to get somewhere
Acting pre-occupied, when someone is talking	Go on, I am listening, I can multitask and by the way your topic is not that interesting. As soon as it is interesting I will stop doing what I am doing and will look at you.
Not looking eye to eye when talking	Sign of nervousness or sign of thinking hard while talking. In some culture looking eye to eye can mean competition.
Eyes looking on the left hand side (up or down)	Generally perceived as, trying to recollect the events from the memory.
Eyes looking on the right hand side (up or down)	Generally perceived as, trying to fabricate the story.
Looking at a cell phone multiple times	Your topic is not that interesting.
A sarcastic smile or a smirk	I know more than what you know, the way I like to call it "Yaa Right"
Un-necessary nods	Yes I am listing, go on; or actually I am just nodding my head but I do not understand what you are trying to say

Listening with very intense look and then putting hands on faces to refresh-self	What did you just say, sorry I could not understand; or the way I like to call it "Sorry I lost you, somewhere in the discussion". This could also mean disbelief in what you are saying.
Looking around, literary glancing at other things when talking	Not interested in your discussion, but yes I can listen and understand what you are saying.
Change in pitch of the tone	Getting involved in the discussion, high pitch might also mean trying to make a point.
Sudden use of different or native language in the discussion	Wait a minute, I am trying to make a point here; why are you not listening to me
Raising eyebrow	Expressing doubt or interest; the way I like to call it "Good I have your attention now"
Rolling Eyes	Oh god, not this message or scenario again

Figure 5

These micro-messages are further sub-divided into micro-inequities, micro-affirmations, micro-aggressions or micro-engagements.

- Micro-inequities are the negative micro-messages that an individual produces or shows (eg. a sarcastic smile or smirk as described above).
- Micro-affirmations are the acknowledgements which make individuals feel respected (e.g. after passing through the door, keeping the door open for the person right behind you and not banging the door on them).
- Micro-aggressions are the signs of slight aggression in a discussion (eg. raising eyebrows as described above).
- Micro-engagements are the micro-messages that show that interest in the discussion is still maintained (eg. looking around, looking at the cell phone or watch as described above).

The micro-messages described in this book are just limited to the topic of "understanding the agenda". While we focus on all types of micro-messages, the primary one we will work on is **"Micro-engagement".** As long as a sign of being engaged in the discussion is turned on, we will continue to work on understanding the agenda and the negotiation. As soon as you see the "disengage" micro-message, that would be the trigger to change the technique.

While most of these micro-messages can be generalized, there are a few of the micro-messages that depend on the ethnicity or origin of the person you are dealing with. In Western culture if you do not make direct eye contact, it is considered rude or not attentive; however in Asian culture if you DO indeed make direct eye contact, it "might" be interpreted as threating or trying to show your power or superiority. In certain countries, while a firm handshake is treated as normal and shows that you have confidence, in Asian countries it can also be treated as showing superiority. You need to collect these micro-messages as a "Databit" and include it in your homework, to be processed later when you are organizing the data. There is a chapter in this book that talks about instincts and studying the instincts carefully; it will help you get to the data gathering process better. So where do we go from here? Before we get to the actual understanding of the agenda of the person and the circumstances, the next chapter will help you organize the data that you just finished collecting.

Key Learnings

1. Gather and organize data effectively.

2. Understand micro-messages to understand the agenda.

Chapter 5

Connecting the Dots

Making the connection is a crucial step to success. There are two types of connections referred to in this book. One is connecting the dots, which is putting things in perspective, and the other one is being connected to the person you are speaking to or working on, trying to understand the agenda. In this chapter we will be talking about connecting the dots. So what is connecting the dots? As kids we had assignments or games where we had to take a pencil and mark a line from point 1 to point 2, then from point 2 to point 3 and so on. The end result of connecting these dots would be a picture or object. I have a vague memory of the first lion I drew by connecting the dots, not because it was my first lion but because someone made a comment: "Look, even after connecting the dots, your lion does not look like a lion." I wish we had easy access to cameras then so that I could have taken a picture of that lion I completed. But yes, that is what I call connecting the dots. We get clues but at times we are unable to put them together, just like the lion I described earlier. The lesson learned from the lion example is this: If you do not connect your dots properly you cannot complete or see the big picture or make any sense of the situation you are in, even if everything is right in front of you. Why is this step crucial in understanding the agenda? Knowing the big picture gives you the upper hand and the perspective of understanding the "why" of the behaviour you are seeing. As the wise say: "half knowledge is dangerous". The more I have seen life, the more I can relate to this statement. For me, a big learning from this statement is that I put all my energy to get the facts. Sometimes when I put the facts together or as I say "connect the dots", I get a realization that I was about to make a wrong judgement. That's ok!! We are human and we all have made mistakes in our lives. Some realize it and some don't—maybe they did not try connecting the dots then or maybe one did not have enough data to make a judgement or choice. In understanding the agenda, connecting the dots is crucial to get the big picture.

Where else would connecting the dots help? I think there is one more scenario where connecting the dots is important—it will help you decide if this battle is worth fighting for. In the end, it is your need that is making you go through this pain of connecting your dots, and helping you look at the big picture. Making the data you have collected talk to you, creating a science of your data, gives you necessary facts to take important decisions. Before you apply the knowledge you have gained by connecting the dots there are other factors which you need to understand. This will help you complete the story. There might be some battles which are not worth fighting for but how would you know if your story is not complete?

People reach conclusions very fast. At times, even before knowing our need, before understanding the pros and cons of a situation, just based on a few stereotypes we jump to hasty judgements.

The first 30 seconds of any interaction are very crucial. The next 2 minutes is the processing time. After 3 minutes one thinks that they have a good understanding of the articulation. After 4 minutes it is facial expression time—this is for people who love reading body language. We talked about "micro-messaging" in the previous chapter. Watch out for the micro-messages. It just could be someone not directly looking at you when talking with you, or continuing to work on what they are working, while trying to talk to you. The idea or the message they are trying to give is "Yes, I will listen, but what you are telling me is not important enough" or "I don't want to give you the importance of looking at you." These indications should tell us if this is a good time to get to the actual topic or whether we should just ponder more, know the person more as this is not the correct time. After the first 5 minutes one has, by and large, made up the mind to either continue the discussion or start looking for excuses to stop it. Treat these 5 minutes exactly as you would handle a quick haggle or bargain. If you are doing your job well, spending enough time on understanding the micro-messages on the interest level of the individual you are dealing with then it would be easy to make a decision on what your next steps should be. If the final analysis is that the person is not captivated a call needs to be taken on whether this is the correct timing of the discussion.

To further explain the point, let me give a personal example. A very senior executive was visiting our office in one of the multinational organizations I worked for. The individual had recently joined the organization and was visiting us for a week to understand the capabilities we could provide. As a general rule we would schedule our standard set of presentations and if there was further interest, we would then take on the discussion at a granular level. This would completely depend on the executives visiting us. During our standard presentation the executive expressed further interest in understanding what we do. However, when asked how we would connect again, the answer was standard: "Please look at my schedule and see if there are any openings." Now to "understand the agenda", even if I could see the openings on his calendar how would I know the exact level of interest the person had? I looked for an open slot on his calendar and booked a meeting for 7 minutes. The Sr. executive was surprised to see a 7 minute meeting maker. I was there on time as the meeting started with the purpose of understanding the interest level. The same rules applied: first

30 seconds of greeting, next 2 minutes of understanding, and then the body reading started. The Sr. Executive continued to work on the machine as the discussion continued. While responding to the emails the individual would look up for a few seconds and then continue with further responses to emails. I kept going, trying to ensure that when I did set up a true follow-up I would cover exact topics of interest. The only responses I got were a few nods. It was clear that the interest which was shown during the standard set of presentations was merely curiosity and nothing more. My 7 minutes ended. I promptly stood up, thanked the individual for the 7 minutes. My needs were not high enough to make a further pitch as there was no interest shown. I left the ball in their court. Passing my visiting card, I indicated if there was further interest he could have his Executive Assistant set up time on my calendar. As I did not see any zeal from the individual it was no point trying to force further discussions. All I would do there was waste their time and mine. The discussion ended there. Just due to my diligence of taking the 7 minutes, I was able to save time for both of us.

What happened next was very interesting. Since the Sr. Executive also understood the purpose of the 7 minute meeting, he did contact me but only when there was a real need at his end. Later, we did do business together. However, during the 7 minute meeting we both understood clearly that the timing was not right.

To decide whether to continue or stop, give these 5 minutes a lot of importance. If your agenda is to do a quick haggle just so that you can close a deal, then you need to spend these 5 minutes merely negotiating. My recommendation is: take the time because if you show or tell your "need" even accidently before these first 5 minutes, you have already started to lose the battle (unless you are trying a technique "give more take everything" listed later in this book). In this 5 minute study also watch out for "the easy sell" syndrome described later in this book as well.

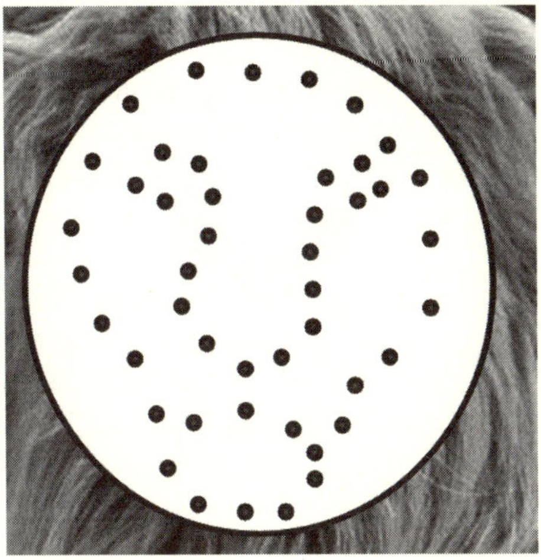

Figure 6

Key Learnings

1. Connect your dots to see the complete picture.

2. The first 30 seconds of any interaction are very crucial.

Chapter 6

Human Connections

Let us now talk about the most important connection—the human connection. Human connections are sensitive but powerful.

For any result, whether positive or at times even negative, the human connection plays a big part. For the human connection to succeed, just try to be YOU. The reason why this fails is that not everyone does this. Even if you try to be yourself what if the person you are talking to does not? So joke or lighten up the situation and don't get caught up in it yet. We need to set the stage before we try handling the situation. If we get into discussions before we have made that connection then there are chances that it might fire back. Sometimes it might work but no guarantee. Getting the connection right is very critical.

Have you ever noticed that sometimes you meet a stranger and start to talk, and you are able to relate to the person, probably understand the person or their perspective? Then there are times when you feel you don't know what this person is talking about? You have no clue. That is because we are unable to relate to them or understand their perspective. That is connection.

My father, who was a genius in Mathematics, always gave this example of "neighbourhood". It was one example which easily resonated with me and most of his students as well. You are at a restaurant with your office colleagues, you see someone from the same street you live in, you wave and you introduce that person to the colleagues around you as your neighbour. Now imagine you were visiting your office in a different city. In the evening while having dinner with your colleagues, you see someone from your own city. The person might not be living on the same street as you, but a few blocks away. However, you wave and call him a neighbour. While visiting your office in a different country, when you see someone from your own country you end up call him a neighbour. The idea that my father wanted to express is "neighbourhood" is a "relative term" used to connect. Connection is very important so one needs to know a good way to figure out the human connection in negotiation.

Connection plays an important role but not exactly during the negotiation. Remember the golden rule: "Everyone has an agenda".

The place where connection is going to help you is in handling things before and in the aftermath of the negotiation. It might help you get a soft corner during the negotiation or may be, help make tough discussions not look that tough. It's like keeping a shoulder ready if you lose or offering your's to someone else. My observation has been that if the connections are made right then they stay on even much after the actual negotiation is done. The questions to understand the agenda become easy now since you have made the connection first and know what the soft corners of the individual are, eg. in which state would that individual loosen up and remove the "mask" from their face to be themselves? This is just the start of the connection; don't draw any conclusion just yet.

Key Learnings

1. ***Human connections are crucial in understanding the agenda.***

Chapter 7

When Tyre Meets the Road

This is one of my favorite topics. No matter how well the tyre is tested before, the actual test of the tyre is when it touches the road in real life condition. If it's a car tyre no matter what quality material it is made from or what indigenous techniques were used to make it, when it gets mounted on the car and when the car is in motion on the actual roads it is supposed to be driven on, only then is the true test performed. In our case the tyre is us and the road is real life scenarios where we use the techniques. So you did the homework, you have all the clues and data points. Have you linked them together? Now what? Well, it's time to test it using one technique at a time or maybe multiple techniques at once. But wait! I have not explicitly told you what the techniques are, have I? Here is what I want you to try. In any scenario which you are in, or rather, stuck in—start your homework. Collect your clues.

I was approached by a friend who had read this. He said, "The only scenario I have at hand is that my kid does not eat well." I said, "Perfect, let's use that one." Any situation is fine as long as you can do your homework. In this scenario the homework I asked him to do was to find out if there was a time of the day when his kid felt like eating. Is there a preference for some type of food? Are there distractions around him when he eats? Where does he sit to eat? When I asked him these questions he looked at me and asked, "What are we trying to solve here, so much data to be collected?" I had to remind him of the scenario at hand—his kid did not eat well. There were two choices, both very simple. One, "try to fix it" or the other, "leave it alone", and here is the good news; both the choices are in our hands and we need to decide which one to choose.

Unfortunately for me, in the scenario we just talked about, when I started asking the questions it daunted him that distractions was the cause that he was going to find and maybe he had already thought of a solution, which meant I could not try any of the techniques with him.

"When tyre meets the road" is one of the critical parts of this book. If you have all the data and you put it into practice what you might find out as soon as the discussion starts is "oh my god, I need more data points and my homework is not enough." Or "I got more than what I was really hoping to get without any negotiation—so why did I do this research?"

The reality is crude but that is the only truth that we all need to deal with.

You can take time to organize the data collected with the "if-then-else" scenarios. However, my recommendation would be, if the stakes are high and if the need is high as well then this would be helpful. Going to a flea market with so much research would not be a good use of time. So practise judgement.

Another key observation I have is that here it is critical to "understand the problem statement". We will be covering the problem statement a little later in the book.

A good way to organize your data is to use a Fishbone (also called cause and effect) Diagram. Where you start with the problem statement at hand and ask questions to understand the problem statement.

For our example let us create a fish bone diagram. While it is one of the simplest examples we can use to get started on understanding the diagram, the idea is to help with conceptualizing how it is done.

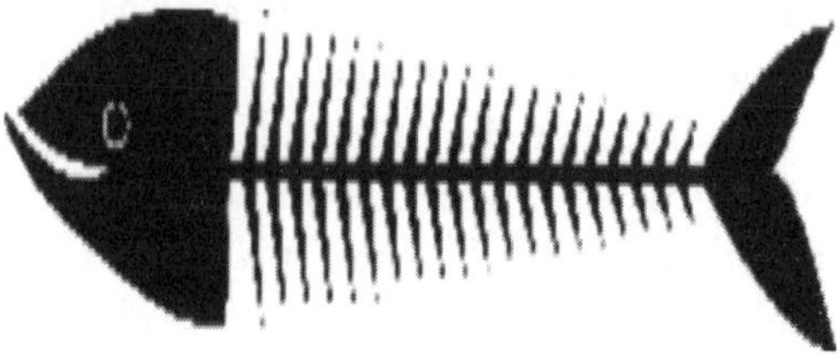

To create a Fishbone Diagram follow the steps mentioned below:

1. Agree on the problem statement (in the earlier example, "the kid is not eating well"). This problem statement will be at the centre of the diagram. Draw a circle around it and draw line arrows running towards it.
2. For our homework now ask the questions around the cause of the problem statement.
   a. *Is there a specific time of the day when the kid eats well? (time category)*
   b. *Is there a preference for a type of food? (items category)*
   c. *Are there distractions around him? (environment category)*
   d. *Where do you sit to eat? (environment category)*
   e. *Who feeds the kid, does the kid eat well with someone? (people category)*
   f. *Does the kid eat initial few bites well and then stop? (quantity category)*
3. The categories will now form the branches from the main arrow.
4. Continue to ask the "Why" question here which would help you get to the intent in the main problem statement.

In the example used above, since the solution daunted my

friend we did not get to the resolution stage. However, if we had to solve it we would have drawn the Fishbone as under.

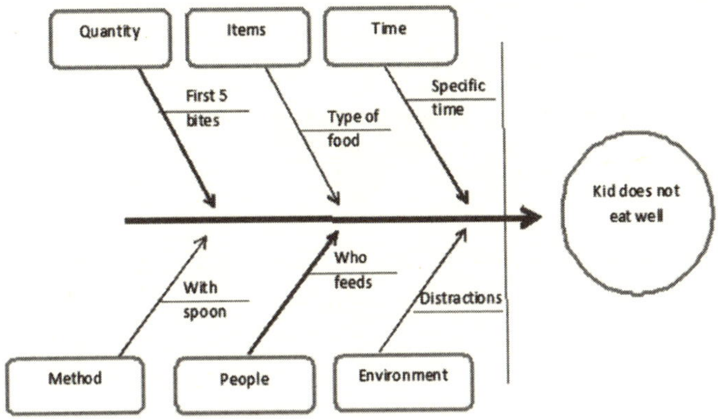

Figure 7

Key Learnings

1. *Test the data collected in real time scenarios.*
2. *Use a Fishbone Diagram to organize your data.*

Chapter 8

It's Never Win-Win

All our lives we have been told look for win-win situations. Whenever we try negotiating it just looks like someone else always wins and we always lose! So where is the win-win? Let me break the myth today.

There is no win-win.

Think about this situation Mr. lucky person!! All of a sudden all your terms are acceptable, you start to feel that the negotiation is going in your favour, you get the comfort that the road is now easy, you start to feel lucky and BAM!! The reality kicks in; all along they wanted you to ***feel*** lucky.

If someone is giving in, there can be multiple factors. You are an easy target or since you are way off it does not matter if the other person gives you a little because overall it's their win. The key to remember here is:

What goes around comes around.

What has that to do with win-win? You let a little go and so will they; you let a lot go and so will they. This might not always be true. However, I have often seen this happen. I start off by giving something away in the negotiation, and then give a second thing away. They start to feel: Wait, he looks motivated, we need to throw in a few things too. A typical scenario in this case would be "bargaining", especially for something big enough. Here are some examples:

1. Bargaining for the price of a house or car you want to buy.
2. Deciding on rent you are willing to pay.
3. Deciding the salary you are ready to accept or willing to pay someone.
4. Fixing the price of a contract you are negotiating.
5. Paying severance package to someone while saving the image of the company.
6. Creating costing sheets based on requirements gathered.

In each of these cases where you have more than one item to negotiate, you can let go a little to gain a little depending on how well you understand the other individual's needs. As I said, there is no guarantee on this one, but it has worked for me in the past.

Why do I then say it's not win-win? Finding a win-win is really tough because you are not sure what a win for the other person would be. While your need is clear and you know what your win is, you would still hope to get a little more than your win. I would recommend that you keep the "hope high", when you start. Start big, then come down to what you want to really get to. This way you are sure to eventually get what you are looking for. Win-win also means you win and so do they. Here the research or data collection normally helps to understand what they are looking for. Look at the past records, which will give you some idea as well. In the end, all is well that ends well, so keep the end in mind, and again I will emphasize: **Keep your need in perspective.** If you get everything but not your need it would not be worth negotiating for, or the negotiating you did would not be fruitful.

I remember a very old scenario. I was in the US working for a multinational company. Due to the nature of the work my teams did, the company had provided us with "two way pagers" to communicate after hours on urgent work-related issues. My spouse and I were expecting our first baby. One evening we were taking a walk in the neighbourhood, having discussions about what to expect and the way our life would be changing soon, when the pager started to beep. I pulled out the pager from the case saying "the offshore teams must be up now" and started to read the message. It happened to be my immediate boss. The message said there was an issue with one of the software applications my teams supported. It needed immediate attention, and while my team member was already engaged, they needed me on the discussion as well.

We used conference bridges to communicate, a common number everyone dials, with a unique pin and depending on the type of the bridge 10 to 50 people can communicate with each other. While it sometimes became a mess, normally if the bridge was controlled well it did become a good communication medium.

While, technically, my spouse and I were talking a walk, I was busy reading the message on the pager, being on the conference bridge answering queries or asking questions to resolve the issue at hand. At one point I looked at my spouse. She understood that I had to run back home so that I could connect my machine as there were a few changes which I had to do to the application. My spouse told me, It's ok! You run back home. She would follow me obviously at her pace. As I started to walk at a faster pace the gap between my spouse and me increased. Leaving my spouse to walk alone in the state she was in made me feel uncomfortable. However I still walked fast, eventually creating a distance between us where I could still see her. A fear developed in my mind. I remember saying to myself, "Is it really worth it?" Today, I don't even work for that company anymore. I left my spouse alone to walk when she probably needed me the most by her side. It was a good discussion we were having before the pager beeped. That moment of my life will never come back, so again, was it worth it?

Someday I want to stop and say I got a win-win when it comes to work-life balance. I am at times too dedicated to work and lose out on the golden moments of life. It definitely boils down to the need of the time. We are so focused on trying to get a few things right that we miss out on the "true" things which have to be right. Now when I look back at the stages of my life, I feel that I have missed out on some real golden moments. So even in this race against time for me, I cannot say I got a win-win. This would be one place where I will ask you serious questions. Did you get win-win in life?

A friend of mine once told me a good statement on work-life balance: "You work till you are 60 years old, and then you have your remaining life to balance."

Did you achieve what you are passionate about? And were able to satisfy everyone that you cared about? If you did, I want to talk to you. Not because you will be a great case study but because you have figured out what your real "need" is; that data would be good for the world to know.

If you get to a win-win situation or if you think you achieved win-win, that's good. Stop and enjoy that moment since it's just life. If you feel you lost some to gain some, sure, still enjoy the moment.

So does it all then boil down to the need? I think it does. The key is finding your need, and then give it all you have got to fulfil that need. This looks good on paper, feels nice when you hear and think about it. The interesting part is, how would you implement it?

Being reasonable is the other side of this coin. When I talk to people about their need, and when we discuss the need, sometimes I feel like the need is beyond the reach in a short time-frame. If you come up to me and say my need is to be the president of a country and you have not even participated in a single election, what answer do you expect from me? Being reasonable also means being practical. You can achieve what you want to achieve, and yes, while everything is possible, it takes time, energy, and resources to make things happen. So, when I talk about win-win I want to ensure that your win-win situations do include being reasonable. For me, reasonable equates to being practical. That might not be true for everyone; remember one size does not fit all. So you will have to decide what is reasonable from your perspective and make sure you have that in your back pocket to help you complete your negotiation.

So, does win-win only mean you give some and so do they. Nope, not always. There might be a scenario where your need and the need of the other would be completely opposite and they would be complementary more than contradictory. Thinking of an example here, say you want to buy a house desperately and a builder is trying to dispose of his houses desperately as well. The reason for the deal not closing is both individuals do not meet at the numbers they have in mind; however there is desperation to close. This would be a negotiation where one should try the win-win situation. You raise the bar a bit and let them lower the bar a bit as well. If you have understood the desperation, chances are they would lower the bar. Share your research with them to make sure the individual understands that you know their desperation.

When you raise the bar, how would you know the needs of the person in front of you? Before we get to analyze the need of the person let us try to understand the different perspectives individuals bring to the table. You might get a true win-win situation if both of your winnings are complementary, whereby we find the common agenda or common need. If you target a common need then yes, you will have win-win. But how do you know for a fact that the person did not tailor his needs to make you look like a winner? So, in a nutshell, if you achieve your need, and you were able to give something to the other individual consider it win-win, because technically, there is no win-win!

Key Learnings

1. There is no win-win situation.

2. Getting what you want boils down to knowing your real need.

Chapter 9

Everyone Has an Agenda

First, let us understand the basic mentality of human beings. It would be mostly true to say everyone has an agenda (note that I said mostly, not claiming that everyone has an agenda!). Some people have a clear agenda; some just don't have a clear one. It's not a bad thing to have an agenda. It is not necessary to attach a negative connotation to the word agenda; some agendas could be to just help other people who are in need. The agenda could also be called "WHY". Why does someone do what they do? We as humans have a few characteristics which do not change.

Have you looked at an individual and thought, Wow this person looks so snobbish? Think again. Was the person snobbish? Or just very focused on their agenda? Since you did not fall within the agenda, you got the snobbish response.

The key is getting to know the agenda. If the agenda is understood well, we would be in a position to understand, "WHY" this person is behaving in a particular manner. If one understands the other individual's agenda, imagine how easy negotiation would be. We wish we could read minds, but while normal human beings can't read minds, we can read the body language, voice tone, hand expressions and facial expressions. For example, it is very easy to tell when someone is not interested in talking to you or listening to what you have to say. That would be when someone cuts your thought midway, or talks about something really irrelevant to what you are talking or they don't give you the necessary attention, as in they would continue doing what they are doing while giving an impression of listening to you or will not let you talk at all and continue with what they have to say.

Sometimes this behaviour is intentional, to indicate that they are not interested or focused on your discussion and have better things to do. The other indication, of looking at the watch, is a globally known or perceived fact. If you are talking to someone and the person looks at his or her watch more than twice, the message is that they are in a rush to get somewhere. They are indicating that you should stop since they are not interested in listening. This reaction could very well be just circumstantial but the message is clear.

Ninety percent of the people would not be interested in listening to you. The remaining ten percent don't feel they need any information from you.

I guess you get the point. To know someone's agenda you have to build that trust factor that we talked about earlier. Getting to know the person is a very important facet of any negotiation deal. Make them predictable while you continue to remain unpredictable. The important part here is that all of us have a sixth sense; how much we develop it or use it is up to us. The agenda can be hidden, implied, direct, indirect, or straightforward and well known. The target has to be to get the agenda before we start the negotiation. This category would fall under doing your homework—if you can do the research before the start of negotiation that is great, but most of the times this become a real time job on understanding and interpreting the agenda as a part of the actual negotiation. Some of the known expressions would be frowning, smiling, laughing, crying, or a serious look. The key is to not give out your agenda while trying to learn theirs. Doing the right thing has to be on the top of your agenda. While doing the right thing might have repercussions, try to stick to that because doing the wrong thing will have larger repercussions. Imagine two countries trying to negotiate—there will be so many agendas (mostly hidden). So what do you do when you learn about the agenda? Well, the next key is to use the agenda to your advantage. Now here is a decision for you: do you twist your agenda to match the person's or do you stick with yours? What I can talk about here is how to close the deal; however as we know everyone has an agenda and the agenda might not be to close the deal. The bottom line for this chapter is:

Everyone has an agenda and the effort has to be to know what the other person's agenda is without exposing your own.

A simple technique to hide your agenda is to smile, and by the way a smile also adds to your face value!

While this remains a sensitive topic overall since I am asking you to focus on your agenda to match someone else's, one clear message remains—**keep your need in perspective.** After all, it is still boiling down to your need, isn't it? It is our need that keeps us going; if there were no needs we would probably have, as a race, achieved everything we really wanted so far.

Some people have strong agendas and some not so much. How would you know that? Just trying to know the person better might or might not get their agenda out. What should we do then? I coach people on how to deal with the different types of people we interact with regularly. While every individual is different we can classify people into one of these broad categories as described below:

1. **The Victim:** These are the people who will always portray that everything is happening against them. They are trying to navigate through this world where despite all the odds they are struggling and want everyone to feel sorry for them. These are the people that often "play cold" as described in a later chapter, and often do not listen well. They will listen to what they want to listen to and beyond that everything else does not fall in their agenda.

2. **The "I can handle everything" One:** These groups of people look very confident. Whether or not they have the data they will try to portray a picture of "I can handle it". Always ready to advise, they never will practise what they preach. I have seen a lot of experts fail here as they don't tend to listen well; all they want to do is advise.
3. **The Revolutionary:** Always ready to challenge the system. If they see anything wrong, always stepping up and challenging the wrong or sometimes even challenging the right. Please don't consider the people in this category as cynical as they might sometimes appear. Have you observed the folks that quibble? It is this group.
4. **The Smarter One:** I also call them the manipulative one. Always calculating, every step they take has an agenda. Like playing chess with life. All moves are well calculated and they would want to navigate through the system their way; right and wrong do not have a meaning. They fall under the "It's my way" described in later chapters.
5. **The Helper:** These groups of people feel sorry for everyone and are always willing to help. While the intention is to always help others, they often get carried away and do not see or calculate all the steps like some of the others listed above. They take life as it comes.
6. **The Follower:** There is a huge number of people that falls in this category. Sometimes it's because they don't want to challenge the system, or don't care about the system, or do not have an idea about how to navigate the system. These would be the people who would be easy to guide since they can easily be told what to do and how to do it. They follow what is being told. At times it does become easy to deal with them but at times it becomes very difficult because they have to be told everything and one does not have time to babysit everyone. You have to be very well organized to deal with this category of people.

7. **The Jovial One:** Tend to make the world laugh with their wit. The interesting part is it would be difficult to deal with people who fall in this category. Their brains work on thoughts instantaneously so the number of options in their mind might be more than what would come to you. If you indeed do not fall in this category but have to deal with them, your preparation work increases.
8. **The Slow One:** These are interesting bands of individuals. The people in this category can be confusing to deal with sometimes. Generally we feel that we have to explain the entire scenario to them multiple times; what we don't think about is while we explain the same thing to them multiple times we might end up giving them a lot more data than what we would have given if we were not dealing with "the slow one". Think about it now, you probably ended up giving out your expected end result as well. The person here might not be sluggish; he or she might just want you to believe that they are slow. A person in this category might be processing a lot of permutations while you are explaining the scenarios to them, thereby understanding it better than anyone else or sometimes even better than you.
9. **The Clandestine One:** A secretive group of people who just don't want to share anything. There is a topic that I have covered which highlights "dealing with cold". These groups of people need a lot of trust to open up. However it is not difficult to get them to reveal their needs or agenda. There are techniques listed in this book which will help in dealing with this bunch. The Billiard Shooter concept, for instance, is explained in Chapter 20.
10. **The Contagion One:** I also call this group as the arrogant one. These groups of individuals, do not just infect themselves, but try to influence the masses by contaminating their minds as well. Always negative, they

can never think of any positive situation. No matter what you do for them they always look at the negative outcome of the decision. The system is bad, the organization is bad, the country is bad; they have no special solution but want to complain and influence the society with "negative" thoughts. This group not only "has an influence", they tend to change the "influence" of everyone around them. Have you heard of an "unproductive meeting"? Sounds familiar?

After we designate people into one of the categories listed above, we need to align them into a quadrant model which gives us the ability to understand the capability of the individual. The end goal for this entire exercise still remains "Understanding their Agenda" and "Why they are doing what they are doing". The approach is to put them into one of the four quadrants listed below. However, before we do that we need to understand the Quad Model. For the X axis I consider the "How" and for the Y axis I consider the "What". This would be specific to a particular scenario. People move from one Quad to the other depending on the scenario.

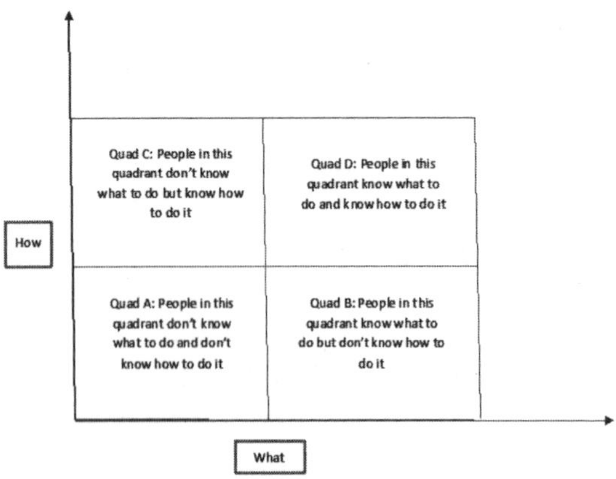

Figure 8

Below is another representation of the same model.

Quad Model	Quad A	Quad B	Quad C	Quad D
HOW	X	X	√	√
WHAT	X	√	X	√

So how does this fit into the model where we get to know the agendas? We use the following table.

Quad A	**Quad B**	**Quad C**	**Quad D**
People in this quadrant are the most vulnerable of them all	The individual knows what to do but does not know how to do it. People in this category will make use of other individuals to get to their motives or agendas.	People in this quadrant are those who get used or taken advantage of most of the time. They know how to do things but don't have a clear direction. Even if they think they know what to do, they would look for acceptance as soon as they make a statement to see how many people are nodding at their thought.	The individual knows what has to be done in a particular scenario and how to do it. These are individuals who know their agenda and know exactly what needs to be done to achieve it. If you fit within their agenda you will be entertained. If you don't, expect the snobbish behavior.

This Quad analysis will tell us the "Why". The basic question we are trying to answer here is: "Why is the person doing what he/she is doing?"

The categories and the Quad analysis need to be aligned together to give us the bigger picture on understanding the agenda. Thereafter, looking at the solutions we can figure out how to deal with them.

So how do we know how to align people into different quadrants as listed here? This would be different for different scenarios so how do we generalize? For generalizing you will need your data collected on the set of individuals you are interested in dealing with. This should not take you years to collect. A few discussions and you should be in a condition to know who falls in which Quad. People might react differently in different scenarios and in some cases you might see that an individual, who is Quad D for a certain situation, falls in Quad A for another. In this case you will also get to know the preference and the comfort zone of the individuals and how much can you stretch them. In my initial days of trying to work with this Quad model, I would always find everyone I was dealing with would fall in Quad D. And I would think either my understanding was wrong or the model was missing something. I would always feel everyone knew how to do things and what they wanted. What I missed out initially was that this is situation based. I am taking an extreme case to explain this.

A person, sitting in the living room of his house, was making a monthly budget on expenditure combining all of the expense his family had and was using a calculator to add them to get the expenditure of his family. (In this case the person knew how the formulas worked and what needed to be done next). Suddenly he saw fire coming out of the kid's bedroom. In a panic mode he kicked open the door of the bedroom. Fortunately there was no one in the room. Seeing fire he ran to the kitchen brought a vessel full of water and threw the water on the fire. What would have happened next? The person in this case knew "How" to get rid of the fire. He threw water on the fire. However, he did not check the cause of the fire. If the fire was caused by a wiring short circuit then throwing water on the fire would not help. This would fall under the situation of not knowing "What" to do especially in the case of emergencies.

The same individual is in Quad D when it comes to budgets, but is in Quad C when it comes to fire related emergencies.

Let me explain using another example. An individual happens to be an excellent individual contributor in the work he does. All of the work which gets assigned is always completed before time and with excellent quality. In fact, he also knows the next steps when it comes to work, which means he is "walking on water" when it comes to being in the role that he is performing. Sounds like a Quad D individual?

With his excellent track record, the corporation that he works for decides to promote him to manager, where he would have responsibilities of managing multiple individual contributors. As a first time manager and dealing with performance, human resource and career planning activities along with technical work where do you think this individual now falls when it comes to being a manager, still in Quad D? He would still remain Quad D for his previous role, however in his current new role he would be a Quad A person, someone who has to be told what to do and how to do it.

Slowly as I started to use this model it began to make sense that not everyone knows everything. There are, I am sure, a few things every individual is great at. But to satisfy your need and to complete your agenda you would need additional help if you don't have what it takes to achieve the need.

Another point after I started to observe was that there are people who know the "how" every time, but are never able to get to the decision power of "what" needs to be done in a particular situation and will always look for expert advice. Even when they make a statement, they would look around the group they are dealing with and see if they get some nods in acknowledgement.

So can we generalize that the people that are always in Quad D are the people who have an agenda? No. Remember what I said earlier: Everyone has an agenda; some are strong some are weak. Also, can we generalize that the people in Quad A have weak agenda? No. They might not know what to do and how to navigate in a particular situation but might know their need very clearly in their mind and might also know that they will have to pass from Quad A to Quad D in that situation to achieve their agenda. Aligning them in Quads gives you a reference of what you are dealing with. With practice you will start to get your data right and find out what agendas people have. Having a strong bond with the person also might get you the agenda but you will not know if that is the only data they want you to have. People sometimes tell me that I am like an open book; that I wear my heart on my sleeve, everyone knows what I think and how my mood is. Well, here is the question I would ask them – just one simple question: You are seeing what you want to see, correct? And you are seeing what I want you to see, correct? They normally pause. Some get it and some don't. We see people and start to analyze them; it's human nature to do that. What this Quad model will do for you is put a perspective and over a few situations help you analyze what you should be focusing on as well.

It's very easy to just always be yourself or you can use a facade that you want the world to see. When sad, it is tough to smile – I get that – but then always having a gloomy face will not help you, will it?

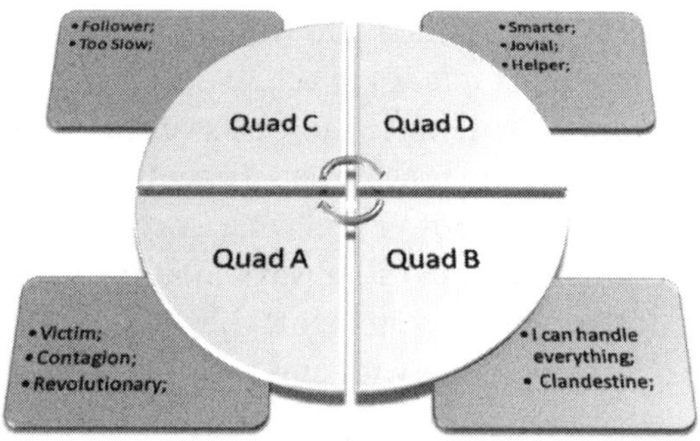

Figure 9

After this, all said and done, you will still see what you want to see, correct? And not pay attention to whether you are seeing what people want you to see or are able to dissect the scenario and have a correct picture? We have a tendency to believe what we want to believe. It's easy and the thought that I am always right puts unnecessary blinders on us. So is everyone bad? No, not really, it is how each of us is framed and wired internally. There is a way to deal with every scenario and every person. Do we really need to study so much about people and know how to deal with them? We go back to basics here: unfortunately yes. We do. We are in a real world and we will meet folks from different backgrounds, natures, characteristics, and thoughts. As long as you breathe you will have to deal with them. Running away from problems is not going to help. Therefore let's try to take it head on. Agreed? I also tend to use this quadrant when I am mentoring someone on their development needs. In the corporate world, when working on performance management this quadrant helps to ensure that we are fair. The overall characteristics of the individual might not change; however, based on their interest, knowledge, willingness, and motivation they might move from one quadrant to another depending on the chosen goal. Also, I would work with them on ensuring that they know what I feel regarding what quadrant they fall in for that particular goal. This helps in setting expectations upfront and also gives them a chance to work on changing quadrants through the year if they want.

I have explained in detail about types of people and how we can categorize them. There is a key to that here. Until one knows what they are dealing with, it becomes difficult to deal with it. I have always believed that it is not the problem that is hard; if you know exactly what the problem is, then solutions are easy and there is a way to deal with that problem. Often we get caught up in trying to find solutions to the perceived problem at hand while we lose focus on understanding the problem statement, as I have mentioned earlier.

I have further expanded our quadrant to help organizations be successful in developing their people managers who have teams to manage, and maturing the individuals within the team to effectively manage the expectations. I call this Management "101". We follow the same quadrant principles of "How" and "What".

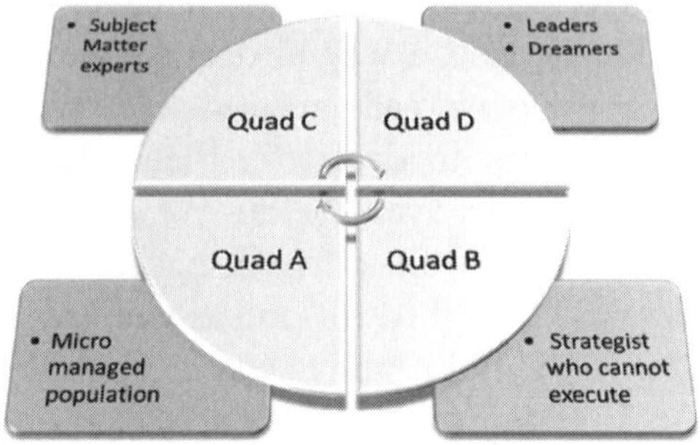

Figure 10

To understand our Management "101" model we need to look at the original quadrant theory we started with.

Quad A: People in this quadrant don't know what to do and don't know how to do it. I like to call this group the **Micro managed population.** This group of individuals always need direction; will always come to you with questions on what the next step should be. They ponder a lot sometimes even before reaching out to you for clarifications.

Example: When someone is either new in a role they are going to play, or just does not have the motivation to learn, or one has been allocated more responsibilities than what they can handle.

Quad B: People in this quadrant know what to do but don't know how to do it. I like to call this group the **Strategist who cannot execute.** While there are brilliant ideas, getting the ideas to reality is a challenge for this group. They can think through on what needs to be done, but for how to do it they will look at you for guidance.

Example: It was late in the evening and my spouse and I decided to go for a drive. We have a few tea vendors who are open late nights and we do visit them often, have a late night tea, take a small ride around the area we live in and get back home. I walked up to the vendor and asked for two cups of tea. The tea vendor, while giving me the two cups, made a comment that the latest cricket team selected by the board was not correct. Cricket happens to be "The Sport" played across the Indian-sub continent and everyone happens to be an expert in this sport. A cricket team comprises 11 players. The tea vendor was making the comment that the selection board did not select the right players for the game. While he could be right in the statement he made, the justification that he had put forth did not resonate with me. I took the two cups from him, paid the money, smiled and walked back to the car.

Have you ever seen a person sarcastically commenting on someone? As if they could fix everything if they had the power. That's the group.

Quad C: People in this quadrant don't know what to do but know how to do it. I like to call this group the **Subject matter experts.** A good group called the "Worker Bee" group. They lack the strategic vision but taking baby steps and doing it consistently is their forte.

Example: In the corporate world we have a group of individuals which falls in the developer community. This group knows how to solve problems "given to them". They would use all possible known technology in the world with ease and fix problems. However, when it comes to identifying existing problems, it falls in the category "not their problem". This statement cannot be generalized as there are developers who also understand the "What". However the numbers there are limited.

Quad D: People in this quadrant know what to do and know how to do it. I like to call them as **Leaders or Dreamers.**

Example: I added dreamers here along with the leaders in this group. They can be either very active and dynamic or lazy because they know it all and no scenario for them is that motivating because its an "I got it" attitude.

The motive behind explaining the model in the context of understanding the agenda is that sometimes the overall agenda is too big for just one person to achieve. When you look for support or for people who can help you achieve your agenda this Management "101" model would guide you better on how you can effectively delegate to achieve your agenda. The key to effective delegation for managers within the corporate world falls in this Management "101" model as well.

It is good to set this expectation and the understanding with your teams. Let us do a few sample exercises so that this thought would resonate with us.. If a person on your team feels that he belongs to Quad D, but you, as his manager, feel that the person belongs in Quad A, imagine the disconnect between the two. You would want to micromanage that team member, but the team member would feel suffocated as he would want to fly free due to his understanding of which Quad he belongs to. If you and that individual have not connected and discussed this, there will be a lot of discontent between the two of you.

We as humans have learned a lot but then there is so much more to learn. Not having an open mind sometimes puts us in a state where we close our willingness to look at others' perspective or even your "true perspective". The idea behind this chapter is to get to understand the players we deal with. The more mature the person, the better the agenda in their mind, which means more planning at our end. That is where we get to the next chapters of "Just Ask" and "Trusting Your Instincts".

Key Learnings

1. *Understand people by classifying them in the categories listed.*
2. *Use the Quad Model to gauge the capability of the other person.*

Chapter 10

Just Ask

At times it might just be good to put all the cards on the table and start with a candid discussion. Starting with: "Here is what I need—what is it that you want?" Looks simple, right? Right!! This is one of the toughest situations. What you are doing is exposing yourself completely when you don't know what the other wants. So when would you use this technique? This would be a technique you would use when the "risk is low". Where you already know a few facts about the outcome or you want to finish the discussion either way and don't care about the outcome. Additionally, your research has given you strong pointers about the type of individuals you are dealing with. You know their agenda somewhat or at least have a high probable idea of their agenda. These are good when you want to set the tone.

I remember a few incidents where I used this technique. The first time I used it in a corporate environment was quite interesting. I was dealing with a vendor team delivering a product for my company. The entire software was being developed by them. However, we needed to manage and control the deliverables. When we got involved for the first time, we did not know a lot about the methods or shortcuts the vendor and their on-site (on-location) teams took. As we started learning about the techniques and got the hard facts around the approach, I pulled in their director in a meeting. Just he and I; we did not include any one else. Such meetings are called "1n1" in the corporate world (aka one-on-one). I made two statements to him. The first one: "You have two choices, do you want to work with me or work against me?" The second statement was: "There is no third choice here." It was "with" or "against" for which I added a few "flavours of clarification" about what it meant "to be with" and what was "against" from my perspective. I then left the meeting room and said that I would be back in 10 minutes for him to tell me his decision. I left him alone, went for coffee and came back in 9 minutes (note: 1 minute less than what I told him). His response, "It does not work this way . . . I have my management to respond to as well . . . our priorities are not aligned . . . I don't want to work against you, but..." I stopped him at "but". This was enough information for me to analyze that if played right he could be a good ally. This told me the "intention" of the person. Now, how did I know that he was not faking? It was the scenario that I put him in. That discussion turned out to be in my favour, it very well could have backfired. Again, from my perspective, I did not have much to lose so the "Just ask" worked for me. I already had the upper hand as I was paying the bills. I did not use the "It's my way" approach here, since I gave him a chance to react. He could have easily come back with the "with" and still continued the "against" approach. But, as I added the "flavours of clarification" it helped put things in perspective. In this approach I used the close-ended questions. Two clearly positioned choices to be chosen from and no third choice.

This approach works well when you have a small stake in the game, the output of which is not going to impact you a lot or your needs are really low. It is a good tool to deal with people that you want to solicit feedback or input from or feel comfortable talking with. "Just ask" could be the "water cooler" or "coffee break" discussion. The question in this scenario can be close-ended where you have worked through the whole scenario in your mind and just want thoughts from a subject matter expert, your mentor, or someone you feel has the intelligence to answer your question. Each one of us has a few unique capabilities but we are human and we don't know everything or are just not that good at everything, hence taking opinions helps. The topic of opinion is covered later in the book in detail.

The "Just ask" question can also be open-ended, for e.g. What is your opinion? Or what do you think we should do in this scenario? Or a typical one that I use in a lot of cases "Thoughts?" In a subject where I want opinions from people and it's more of a direct connect either by e-mail or in a meeting the "Thoughts?" works great. Most of the times people respond directly to me which helps me collate the data and summarize easily. Plus it gives folks a chance to respond freely on what is on their mind regarding the particular subject.

There are times when explicitly asking specific questions helps, but then there are scenarios where open-ended questions work as well.

At times I have used "Just ask" as ice breakers, putting the scenario on the table before the discussion and asking the people for their opinion or feedback in that particular scenario. It helps put things in perspective and also opens up the topics to understanding the agenda of the other person. I have seen a lot of senior leaders in the corporate world use this technique. When a leader manages large teams, the leader does not get to interact with everyone regularly. When they do interact or meet with someone for the first time, as a hall way conversation, "Just ask" works perfect. The employee will straight get to the key thing that is on his/her mind if the question is asked correctly. It really becomes the art of asking the open-ended questions. Open-ended questions are like shooting in the dark but you do end up getting back a lot of valuable information. The responses to open-ended questions might be lengthy so you might have to listen in and probe as needed to get to what is on the person's mind. Remember, we are only trying to get to our needs; the needs have to be kept in perspective.

Practise the "Just ask" technique and add it to the storage unit of the brain for future use. Since "Just ask" can include open-ended questions, the grey matter might still have to be used to process the information and ask the next appropriate set of questions.

Key Learnings

1. *Use the "Just ask" technique when the risk is low.*
2. *Good tool to use when you want feedback or inputs.*

Chapter 11

Trust Your Instincts

Here, "Influence" is a key as we all get influenced easily. Well, we are humans, what else do you expect? Under influence we lose the capability to trust our own instincts. There is no doubt that everyone has instinct. I feel everyone is different when it comes to experience. You have seen the world and interpreted the world like no one else has. The outcome of anything you see would have a meaning in your mind. The storage unit of your brain stores multiple experiences you have gained over the years. This, on a high level, is what I call instinct. The ability to know the outcome of an event based on your own experiences. This would be different for different people, and I would recommend that you trust your instincts more than you trust the influencers. Maybe your instincts have never been right or you have had mixed results and most of the time your instincts have been wrong. I am sure your brain is taking care of processing that information and putting a perspective in your mind. You probably are now scared to use your instincts because you are not sure of the result. In any case, there is no doubt that you have an instinct. If you still have doubts, let's think about this one, a little more. Do you do any basic things on your own? Like climbing stairs? Eating food? Anything your basic nature would do? In the case of climbing stairs why don't you climb 4 steps in one go? In the case of eating food, why do you not eat a few things that your tongue does not like? Something, somewhere rings a bell? These would be your unconscious instincts or what the biological genius would call a reflex action, the ability to perform action without completely being aware of the action. This would be one type of instinct. As explained in Figure 1, this would be the automagic part of your brain interacting with the storage unit.

Let's explore influence and instinct a bit more. When a doctor prescribes the medicine for a particular ailment, the medicine might get you back to the normal state. Do you bother to check on what was given to you? Now if a similar ailment recurs, what is the first thing that comes to mind? Well!! I was given a medicine which worked in the past, let me use it now, it might work again. While you are not positive if it is the same problem, you think you can try the same medicine. This is where you look at the storage unit of the brain and pull out previous experiences.

Another example here: when you are in a discussion with multiple people, you tend to agree with some people and disagree with some. Have you thought why? The thoughts that you tend to agree with are probably similar to your own thoughts, whether they are right or wrong. Additionally, when two or more people talk about what you already have in mind, your thought tends to solidify now that you have a few more people agreeing with you. You would in this case tend to ignore any "flaws" that it would have.

There is an important message in this chapter: While instincts are important we need to groom our instincts to ensure that we are open-minded, so that we can do the right thing. Since this is your need that we are dealing with in the first place, be honest with yourself. Keep no favouritism while working on the instinct.

We focus on how to mature your instincts or in other words what we should remember to ensure we are neutral enough to trust our instincts. A preconceived notion cannot be called instinct and should not be used as benchmark to judge your instinct.

Below are the general categories of instincts. It is important to understand not just the instincts but how to groom them so you can pick up the necessary vibes. The following table needs to be added to the storage unit of your brain:

Instinct	**Example**
Stereotype	Judging someone by religion or appearance
Pre-conceived notion	This has been proved in the past
Agreeing with the masses	Just because everyone is saying it must be true
Incorrect estimation	Over or under analyze the situation
Lucky	When I wear red, I win in casinos
Parental blindness	My Kid is the best, even if he/she misbehaves. It must have been the other kids fault
I know how this works	I do this for living, I am an expert just follow me.
Recently used	Recent incident becomes the reference point.
Line of sight	Only looking at options which are in front of you.
Insurance	Worried about failure, hence choosing the option with least chance of failure
Managing by the seat of your pants	Not enough time to react, misjudging due to lack of time.

Figure 11

Now that we agree that everyone has instinct, what do we do with instincts? Use it of course! When I started to observe my instincts, I realized I had a 50-50 chance of being right with my instincts. On the one hand I was happy that at least 50% of the time I am right. But obviously, 50% of the time I am wrong too. I sat down and thought through on how to increase this ratio to be more positive than negative. I kept track of the moments when I used my instincts or at least thought of the options and output. Next, I kept track of the result, be it positive or negative. For both scenarios I analyzed the reasons why I chose one option over the other. This helped me tremendously. I have now developed a new habit; I promote my own thoughts. By default I make a choice on my instincts and study the results. My observations are for myself and I cannot generalize that it will work for you. But I know for sure what it will do for you. Keeping a track of the results of your instincts will help you get to the facts of what is going wrong with your instincts. I would promote the use of your own instincts versus someone else's influence since they might have an agenda and might lead you on the wrong path. I am sure you will agree with this statement: the only person on the earth who will not lie to you is yourself, for everyone else has an agenda. If you have done your homework well, you have understood the micro-message that you thought you received, then why would you not trust yourself? I am not asking you to be arrogant or not seek advice or not have a tendency to learn more. We don't know everything, so always be eager to learn. Every scenario has a "rational" approach; choose the "rational" approach or the approach which will benefit the situation. Keep your agenda in mind and then decide what would be the right path. The take-away from this chapter is this: while being humble trust your own instincts more than anyone else's.

Key Learnings

---

1. Groom your instincts to ensure that you are open-minded.

2. Everyone has an agenda, so trust your own instincts.

Chapter 12

Energy Factor

When you think of energy factor what comes to your mind? When I think of energy factor, kids are what come to my mind. They have energy to argue (their way of negotiating) or twist you around because they know you love them or sometimes they just want to test your patience.

They have a great tendency to make a cute smiley face and tire you out. This is one scenario where you are happy losing the battle because you want to give a feeling of victory to the other side due to the energy they have. You want to lose or finish the discussion since you don't have the energy. Either way the loss is yours. Having the energy to continue a discussion is an art in itself. However, if overdone, it can backfire. So you want to show the energy and the patience at the same time, where one has to believe that you will not quit no matter what and have enough patience to deal with that scenario without losing the "motto" of the discussion.

People that show a lot of energy are well-respected as long as they can balance the perception with patience. So how do you build energy to negotiate? People come up and tell me that firstly it is boring to negotiate; now you are asking to infuse it with energy? I smile and give them the cold shoulder, which acts as an eye opener. The chapter "Dealing with Cold" deals with how to deal with cold or unfriendly people. Your aim is to "wear out" the person with your energy so that they give in. Your other aim is not to be worn out if you meet someone who has a lot of energy. Serious negotiating takes a lot of patience and preparation if you want to "win". My kid once told me this while we were watching a movie: "**Time flies when we are having fun.**" I paused for a second and thought, Wow, enjoy negotiation and time will fly with energy. Coming out with ideas which can exhaust the person is a trick as well. I call it "moving minimum 4 chess moves in one step". For the people who have played chess, I think you can relate to the scenario; for the folks who have not, my goal is not to teach chess in this book so I will give another example. When there are too many moving parts at one time it becomes difficult to decide on which one we should focus. When you start to change the environment in a rapid manner around the scenario you are dealing with, while you need to have control over what you are trying to change the person whom you are dealing with will take much more time to react. You know the circumstance which you are planning to change, the other person does not. So before someone could react to the change, change more than what you feel they can handle. How do you know how much they can handle? This would be a part of your data collection and learning as you negotiate technique. Making it too much to handle for them will make them cave in; hence if the need is more, the energy needs to be more too. Remember "Octopus" our ally, has 8 arms or should we say legs, and they can move parallelly.

A very good example that comes to mind in this case is the games corporations play when recruiting using multiple interviewers, also called as "panel interview". The only candidate who will survive at the end of the discussion will be the person who has a lot of energy to deal with multiple questions from multiple people almost at the same time. The ambiguity of who is asking a follow-up question or who is going to stop the discussion and change the questions becomes tiring for the interviewee. One of the interviewers might really act tough on questions while the other one might sound soft for the interviewee to fall in the "Good Cop/Bad Cop" trap. Another example here would be a similar type where there is a panel but it would be a team one would interview with. While I was living in Kansas City, US, and looking to change jobs, I had an interaction with the Operations and Site Head called Chris K. He was a gem of a person to deal with. He had briefed me before I went in to the interview that this would be a full day interview. The work place was 2 hours 30 minutes from my home, which was already the concern in my mind before I went for the interview. I left early that morning to reach their office by 9:00 AM; fortunately I did not have an issue finding the place. Chris introduced me to his team and then the grilling started. One discussion after another. At times it was one person interviewing me for 30 minutes or a team talking to me for 1 hour. This went on till 1:00 PM. I barely managed to grab some lunch and we were back in interview mode. This went on till 5:00 PM. Imagine my plight: whilst I had to perform at my best, the discussions were tiring. Had I shown the slightest sign of exhaustion the game would have been over. I left the place at about 6:00 PM, and drove back home for another 2 hours and 30 minutes. Although this was tiring and stressful, keeping the energy level high and doing your homework always helps.

A third example to explain the energy factor is dealing with more than one boss. In the corporate world these days there is one manager that you report to for Human Resource. However, there is a term called "Matrix" managers, people whom you report to for work alignment. The need for high energy here equates back to answering the questions: "Whom should you follow?"; "Where are you getting your assignments from?"; "How do you manage conflicting priorities?"; "How do you gain the necessary trust?"

The idea to be added to the storage unit of your brain in the case of energy factor is "time flies when we are having fun".

Be passionate about what you do. As Gautama Buddha said, "Your purpose in life is to find your purpose and give your whole heart and soul to it."

Key Learnings

1. *The person with higher energy level will eventually win.*
2. *High energy level will help you to tire out the other person.*

Chapter 13

Dealing with the Cold

What do you do when you have cold, cough and are feeling really sick? Eat medicine, fight it out, consult a doctor, or hit the bed and call it a day.

So, what do you do when the person you are trying to deal with is cold? Here the person being cold "does not respond to anything". No explanations, no expressions, no regrets, no promises, and no response whatsoever.

They would just act "Cold". The term, cold-hearted, originated somewhere in the 16th century, however the reactions and feeling probably existed much before that.

The term also originated from cold-blooded animals. These animals cannot regulate their body temperature and hence they become sluggish under certain circumstances. An extreme condition in this case would be schizoid personality disorder; however we are not talking about this extreme condition in the book.

A cold person would be someone who continues to stare at you without any expression. Note this is not even a poker-faced look, this is a blank look; or someone talks to you without any voice modulation as if the message is only limited to the critical things needed. Now, if this person happens to be someone that you don't have to deal with often, good for you. The reason for this chapter in the book is lot of time you do need something important from people that do give you the "Cold" and this chapter would help you break the cold. For making the explanation easy I have also used the word "ice".

Have you had an opportunity to deal with someone like this? How do you break the ice with them? If you have come across someone cold, you will agree with me that this is a tough one. If you have not, either you are lucky or you have mastered the art of breaking the ice. Understanding the agenda of the Cold is complicated. If you give up halfway you will face serious difficulties and it would become an even more difficult scenario to deal with.

There are multiple techniques to break the ice; the first one is trust. You need to work on building the trust and sticking to it. Trust has to be built up to make the person believe that if he opens up there will be no repercussions, no matter what the outcome is. Building the trust takes time and a lot of effort. So you need to keep a few things in perspective and make sure you have answers to the questions you want to ask yourself. Before you get into building the trust you need to be sure that "it is worth it" and our WIIFM or "what's it in for me" is clear in our mind. If the answers to those are visibly clear and you feel it's worth it, then your time starts now.

The other method to break the ice is threat. One thing to keep in mind is that a threat can backfire and the ice can become even harder to break. Threat works in some cases when you can convince the person that the repercussions are serious. Here the person needs to have a stake in the outcome. If the person has no stake in the outcome and you use threat, it is not going to work.

What other techniques can we use when dealing with a cold person? What do you do when you have a cold? Eat medicine, fight it out, consult a doctor, or hit the bed and call it a day?

In our case of dealing with the "Cold"

- Eating medicine would be threat,

- Fighting it out would be building trust
- Consulting a doctor is called "Third play" and
- Calling it a day is called "Let it go"

"Third play" and "Let it go" are covered in later chapters in the book.

When dealing with a cold, whether your condition is improving or not improving, what do you do? You continue to fight it. In this case it has to be clear to the person you are trying to deal with that you have not given up unless you reach the "Let it go" moment. The notion of willingness on your part to continue to understand their agenda needs to be clearly known and very well-articulated. The foundation work of indicating that you have decided to deal with the cold needs be told up front. While you are either trying to build the confidence or trying the threat or the getting a doctor involved, an initial discussion is very critical to set the foundation.

How do you set the foundation? "Remember, you did not start the fire." When trying to help someone with breaking the ice, you will have to make it clear that it is not you that started the fire and all you are trying to do is to help with the effort. Why is this step important? Sometimes one tries to help but the person you are trying to help does not know that. Hence there are negative vibes that start to develop. Questions such as "Why am I asked these questions?" or "How do they care?" start to come up. You can give a "micro-message" of showing that you care. What has also helped me in the past is having one very candid discussion at the start of the effort. Again please note it has to be worth your time and the need for this has to be very high. A clear message which needs to be communicated is:

Don't consider my silence as weakness.

As long as the foundation is set, things should start to fall in place.

Remember, if you use cold to deal with cold it's more than likely to lead to a stalemate or deadlock. Which means you are probably not moving forward from there. On a side note, giving "cold" to "cold" would only work if you let it go soon. People need to understand that you can do it too but you are trying to end the stalemate.

Figure 12

Breaking through the cold could be as difficult as using a chisel (a tool with a cutting edge specially made of metal) to carve your way through an iceberg. You are not sure how much time it will take and even if it gives you way you are not sure of the impact. The iceberg can drop you all the way down to the bottom of that iceberg. Getting out might be difficult. Patience is the key, and asking the right questions is very critical. Catching the right message in time is even more critical in this case. There are a few things which are good if left alone; this could be one of those scenarios as well.

Maybe "Let it go" might be the final outcome of dealing with cold if it takes forever to get rid of the cold. Do you know what "Spiral" model is? And why this is relevant? You want to use your techniques as if you are trying to solve a riddle which starts from small steps achieving the final goal of breaking the ice.

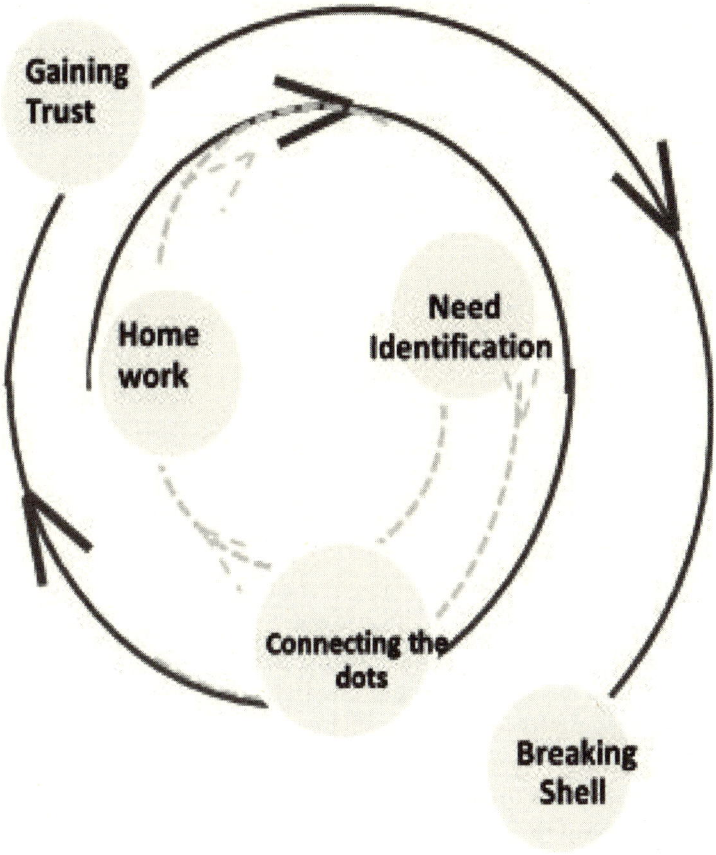

Figure 13

Key Learnings

---

1. *If you use cold to deal with cold, it will lead to a stalemate.*
2. *You can choose to either fight it out or let it go.*

Chapter 14

It's My Way

We can learn a lot about negotiating from kids. If a baby is crying, the first thing you would want to do is get it a pacifier or cajole it so it stops crying. The baby is instinctively crying because something is wrong. Babies use crying as a means to communicate a problem; adults, on the other hand, whine!

All of these symptoms are related to "It's my way". Some people are smart and they know they are smart. Other folks are smart but they just don't know it. So when you see someone trying to negotiate with you and trying the "It's my way" approach, a bell should ring in your head—this fellow is smart at negotiating and knows it. You should be able to tell that you are dealing with a person who has "It's my way" characteristics. And if you tell him he is good at it, that it would be tough to negotiate with him, here is what you just did: boosted his ego.

"Life is a constant conflict between the Humble and the Egoistic". ***I believe for the humble, it's ok to*** **say** ***Sorry but the egoistic always want to*** **hear** ***it.*** So boost their ego and then take what you want. The people in the "It's my way" mode are normally strongheaded and its good for you if they stick with that since people with "It's my way" attitude normally lose big time in the end if you play your cards right. When ego is involved people are working on proving themselves right and proving others wrong. The "halo" should continue to be on your head since people working on proving themselves right get carried away with proving others wrong. What you need to be watching out for is when their "carried away" moment starts. That would be the time to take back what you want. The key element to watch out for is the moment when people start to get "carried" away. They would digress from the end that you have in your mind. Yes, the end still needs to be clear in your head and needs to stay clear till the end (no pun intended!).

When your need is high and you decide that you have to deal with "It's my way" individuals remember that this could be a lengthy process. Let me explain. If your need is high and if, to fulfil your need, you have decided to deal with "It's my way" type of individuals, it might be a long process since you will have to watch for the moment they start to get "carried away". They would begin to move away from your need but on a path to continue proving their point. Only your persistence will improve your drive and help them to drop the "It's my way" attitude. Otherwise there is waiting involved here. What should you do while you wait? Continue to collect the data. "Follow the data" would be a mantra here. We have covered in the earlier chapters the points about what type of data you would need to collect. We did not, however, explicitly list out what data would be needed for "It's my way" types. Your data here would be digging through the history of the individual on when they get "carried away" or what situations could be created so that they get "carried away". There are some negotiation situations that are tricky; dealing with "It's my way" types would be one of those situations. This group of people fall under "I can handle everything" or "Clandestine clan" described earlier in the book. If not required I would not even bother to deal with such folks. But as I said earlier in "Life is not fair", we could end up dealing with headstrong people. Obviously, as in every situation, walking away would be an option but I feel that it should be the last resort.

"It's my way" individuals like to be consulted always while making decisions. The "carried away" moment for them in such an example is when you "help" them achieve the "It's my way" moment. Probe them with specific questions which will make them understand where their advantage could be. This technique is called "spoon feeding". Exactly the same technique that you could choose for a small baby or toddler. You would get the entire meal ready—the same meal that you really want your kid to eat—and then, with appropriate distractions, spoon feed the same to your child.

If you decide to "walk away" it is very good practice to make the people understand that it's not that you are scared to deal with them, but that your needs are not high enough for you to spend time on them. Keep your self-esteem intact even if you adopt "walk away" as these individuals feel happy when you drop the discussion with them. These types of people feel they have won because they always want to win or they always feel that everyone else is not worth anything. In the corporate world we refer to such people as "sycophants", as they like people looking up to them or "licking their boots". They assume that it is they who are paramount and not that they are just playing a role for the company.

These types do not go far in life. Be humble, be yourself and always have self-respect, and keep your eyes on the "carried away" moment. You make your move then and make sure you only get what your "need" is; there is no point for you to be an "It's my way" type. Respect is a feeling that is earned, not demanded, and a lot of us forget that at the end of the day we are humans and so is the individual we are dealing with. As indicated earlier in this chapter, dealing with "It's my way" folks requires a lot of patience.

Key Learnings

1. *Dealing with "Its my way" people can be a lengthy process.*
2. *Watch out for the "carried away" moment.*

Chapter 15

Power Play

What a powerful topic!

When you are dealing with a scenario where power play is involved, this would be one place I would recommend "watch your footprints". You obviously have an option of walking away from the scenario. The walking away option is explained in later chapters. Power play is when you have to deal with people who have the power of decision making and you have to play by their rules. When the stakes are high, for example, related to job or a crucial contract which could make or break you, power play becomes even more crucial. Can you remember such an incident?

For the folks in the corporate world, one of the scenarios that would resonate would be a manager you worked for in the past. Oh yes! I have had my share of power play managers too. Fortunately for me, the people that I am referring to were from the "I can handle everything" group which made my dealing a little easy. But that might not always be the case.

The people that I have talked to about this topic mostly have sour thoughts about it. Why? Because they feel helpless. Dealing with "feeling helpless" is the next topic in this book but in this topic we will handle dealing with power play. You will recall that the first chapter was "Identify Your Needs". As explained, this would be a most crucial step when it comes to understanding the agenda and then the actual negotiation. However, when dealing with power play, one additional step is needed: to identify the need of the individual you are dealing with. We did talk about it earlier in this book; however, we will get to the roots of how to identify the need in the case of power play. People in power have needs too. Sometimes their needs include more powerful positions, sometimes they are just working on a mission. In power play, think of it from the other individual's perspective. Sometimes you feel that they are ruthless but at times they might be dealing with someone else's power play as well. So understanding their needs is even more crucial. The same steps that you follow to identify your own needs will have to be followed to identify their's but with a few variations. Gaining trust is important else how would you know their needs? And how would you gain trust? Remember the connection we talked about earlier? **Oh yes!! A lot of things are interconnected.**

In the case of power play, some of the other techniques listed in the book help too. One can use "Just ask". However, if you are indeed talking about your immediate boss in the corporate world, just ask might not be the right option.

An example, especially the case of new corporate managers or new corporate leaders, fits perfectly for this scenario. Most of the times these newbies have a tendency of showing their assumed power by questioning the individuals reporting to them, and it's just because they can. What they miss is that corporate negotiations never happen as individuals. If they don't have a support system from their reporting teams, they would not be in a condition to travel very long alone. People who really show the power play options normally have a lot of dead bodies lying around when they reach a specified milestone in their lives. If a person is a newbie in their role (have really not handled that role before), they are really starting their journey from "Quad A" described in Figure 8. Sometimes it becomes difficult for these individuals to understand that at every new stage in life you have to learn the tricks of that stage.

In the corporate ladder there is a learning curve to get from team leader to manager. And the learning curve is even more steep when it comes to becoming an executive in the corporate world. The individual needs to be educated that with his performance he did make it to the next level of leadership but obviously every stage has a trade of its own to succeed and excel.

Leaving dead bodies will not get you far. Hence another way to handle the power play scenario is to educate the individual who is showing the power play mode. You just have to be careful as the education should not be the first thing that you try on them. Initially you do need to gain confidence, understand part of or if possible their full agenda along with helping them learn the tricks if you already know them.

Besides gaining trust what else can one do when it comes to power play? Let's try something—look at your right hand; now look at your left hand. What do you see? Nothing really!! Well, you need to look for the right hand and left hand of the people in power play. Not literally, of course! Please don't catch their left and right hand and try to analyze that, it might actually get you in trouble!

The left hand and right hand here signifies people who "influence" the "influencers" or in our case the power play. Get to know the needs of these people through their "influencers". While it is difficult to understand some people; it is not impossible. There is one line that I used in the first chapter: "Life is not fair—get used to it." No one said dealing with power play is going to be fun or going to be easy. We have decided to take on this challenge, hence I am giving you all the necessary points needed to complete it.

What else would you be looking for in collecting this data? Hacking into their brains would solve all problems but that is easier said than done. At times collecting data for such individuals might just mean talking with all their acquaintances to see if there is some information that you can get. Be careful when you try this scavenger hunt technique, it should be silently done without giving out hints on what you are looking for.

Key Learnings

1. *Identify the need of the individual you are dealing with.*
2. *Gain the confidence of the other person to understand his agenda.*

Chapter 16

Feeling Helpless

There are times when we think things are not under our control. It's a common feeling. You want things going one way and it turns out things are going exactly in the opposite direction. Take road accidents, for instance. No driver has an intention of having an accident. But it happens. Things happen. What can you do?

Change Attitude—it's all a matter of mind, if you don't mind it does not matter.

So what's your game plan to handle the Feeling Helpless stage? If you think you have tried everything possible then the best thing is to stop and think through the entire scenario. We try to get things easily and very fast. But as we have already said, "Life is not fair—get used to it." Things may or may not happen the way you want them to and it's ok!! If you quit when you feel helpless, remember it's over. But if you persist then it's not done until its "done". There are ways out of every scenario. If you have tried—try harder. One clear message that comes out of this one is "There is always a way out". There are no dead ends while you are alive. While you move from feeling helpless to the "Let it go" mode, highlight the impact of that decision to yourself and the person you are dealing with. What I have observed is that while it is critical to have your self-respect intact it is also critical to articulate the "impact" of your decision. This would be one way of getting out of the Feeling Helpless mode. If the need is high on the other side this would be a time for them to understand that you are close to "Let it go" and that once you let it go, it's over!

I have sometimes expressed my Feeling Helpless moment with anger. Sometimes I would just show anger so that people would leave me alone. When feeling helpless, this is a way to say, Not right now, I'm not in a good mood, or Leave me alone or I need to think. The only catch with anger is that you want to *show* anger but not *be* angry. That is where a thin line needs to be drawn. You want people to understand that you are not happy with the situation. It is your right to let them know you are not comfortable with that situation. Unfortunately, when someone shows anger, in response people have a tendency to make that person even angrier. This is my litmus test during the Feeling Helpless mode. If I am angry and the people I am dealing with try to make me angrier, my litmus test indicates that it is best to avoid those people then and in the future. But as I said in the previous chapter, everyone has an agenda, and the sooner you understand this the better. Feeling helpless is a tough one, since it's like you have given up. If you give up there is nothing more for you to do. I would recommend one thing here—change the circumstances. Whenever I feel helpless, I start by analyzing what I can change. Can I change the people, the environment, the scenario, the situation, or myself? So far I have been successful in finding one or two things that I can change or influence. Bingo!! I am back in business after that change. Of course, it is easier said than done. Like I said, this one is a tough one. So how do you go about it? When you get into Feeling Helpless mode, first think of options. Try not to stay in the helpless state for a long time. The key message here is "change something". It is easier to change the environment than to change yourself. We are conditioned in a particular manner and over the years we become rigid. If you can successfully change yourself without any compromise, tell me how you did that; it would be good for other people to know how to come out of this situation too!

Feeling helpless is a frustrating and tough state to be in. You are there because you have most likely tried a lot of options and none have worked. Everyone is smart, we have to respect that. If someone has pushed you in a corner, either they were smarter than you or you caved in easily. The way I like to look at things is a little different: **I don't feel helpless unless I make myself helpless.** I never take the first punch, but normally the last one is always mine. Maybe that's my nature. I also believe that what goes around, comes around. Hence, as far as possible, I don't try to manipulate the situation. I know it's not a good thing. However, if someone tries to corner me, I definitely try to wiggle out of it and stay away from getting into the Feeling Helpless state. However, keeping a grudge never helps; it will hurt you more than you know as described in the later chapter, "I always lose when I am angry". The sooner you get that, the better. Everything will not happen the way you want it to. If at every moment you are going to feel depressed or helpless, you are not going anywhere in life.

Humans have a name for everything and the wise people call this state "depression" or "getting into depression". What is depression? A state of depression starts with either anxiety or stress and can be traced back to childhood. Obviously, if someone has entered the state of depression then consulting a psychologist or a psychiatrist would be a better option to bring the person out of depression. The purpose of this book is to prevent an individual from entering the state of depression.

Feeling helpless is a state that you inflict upon yourself. You are not the first or the last human dealing with difficult situations. Remember, no matter how great your solution is, there is obviously a better one. So look for that yourself. The only true friend you have is you and the only worst enemy you have is you. The question that arises is: How do you want to deal with yourself? You could, of course, think of thousands of reasons to pity yourself but it won't help you. Everyone has problems—really everyone does. The question is, do you make yourself feel helpless or try to come out of it? If you fall in a ditch, a big ditch, and there is no one around, what will be the first thing you will do? You will try to come out of it, won't you? You will be surprised, when I ask this question to people, I receive interesting answers. Some folks start with: "Well, I am not that strong, how can I come out of it? Will there be something available to catch so I can come out?" I have to go back with a statement: "You need to have trust in yourself and the only one, really, **the only one who can help you, is You.**" It might be easy for a few folks but it is not easy for a lot of us. The other message which I called out earlier is **I only lose when I really want to.** If I don't give up no one can make me. Since this is a real tough one you will see the same message repeated over and over and over again. Keep your head in the place where it belongs— neither too high, neither too low, look at yourself in the mirror, keep your need in the back of your mind and make a determination that you will come out of this situation. It's not going to be easy, but until you try you will not know. If it was really easy you would not be here in the first place, so you probably just needed a small push. When you look back at that situation you want to smile at yourself with the "silly me" smile. It's these small smiles that make life interesting; we have to live in the present and deal with the present situation. So if you ever feel helpless again in life, open this book, read this chapter one more time, get a hold of yourself and "Jump"—you will come out of it. Think about all the good things you have had in life—getting a decent meal, for instance, is also a good thought—we normally don't think about small joys in life. Remember you are in this situation because you chose to be in it. Always keep the "need" at the back of your mind. If your needs are taken care of then you don't need to feel helpless as there is nothing to feel helpless about. If your "needs" are not met yet then start with a positive thought of how you will satisfy them. Staying in the Feeling Helpless state will never get you the "need". So you will have to either change the situation or change the "need".

I would recommend the first option, which we also covered earlier, of changing the situation. You, and only you, have the power to influence the state you are in, and no one in the world can help you if you really don't want to help yourself. People can influence your decisions, your mood, and your environment but in the end it's all about "you" and only "you", since it's your need that has brought you in this situation in the first place. The reason we have been stressing on this and repeating this point in this topic is that for you to change, or change the situation, you need to keep reminding yourself that "this is not where I want to be in life" and something's "gotta change". Feeling helpless is not a state you want to be in for long and the wise call this state "depression". Please grow up!! Be the adult that you were meant to be. You have a mind and the mind will sway the way you want it to sway. So think of the small joys you have had in your life and smile. Be thankful that you have what you already have and SMILE when feeling helpless. Remember that a smile drives people crazy in a positive and negative manner, which works to your advantage.

One last time . . . when in the Feeling Helpless state—"JUMP". The dictionary definition of jump is "push oneself off a surface and into the air by using the muscles in one's legs and feet" or "move suddenly and quickly in a specified way". Sometimes the solutions are very easy; however we have a tendency to overcomplicate everything. In the feeling helpless state you need to jump from that state into some other state, else you will be in that state for the rest of your life. Help yourself because no one else will and remember "life is not fair—so get used to it".

Key Learnings

1. There is always a way out.

2. No one can help you if you don't want to help yourself.

Chapter 17

Similar Poles Repel

This is a very simple topic but a very critical one. Human beings behave like magnets. When making buddies we feel comfortable with people who have similar thought processes or similar ideas. However, when we negotiate, we have a fair chance to get the winning edge if we are not negotiating with a person of "similar thought". We try to do our best in negotiation and do not realize that we are talking to or negotiating with a person who is just like us. In this technique you need to awaken your inner octopus to change multiple approaches, so that you try to get an edge over the other individuals.

Think about this one as: If you are easy to work with, I will be stubborn. If you are stubborn then I will be easy to work with. My need is to complete the discussion with a result in my favour. I will change my techniques to adapt to yours. Being a stalwart with a stubborn person is not going to help since all you will do is waste your energy and your need will still only remain a need as you would have not accomplished it. Your mission is to satisfy your need, and not to have tons of enemies in life. Your inner octopus needs to understand what is critical when the "need" is high.

Figure 14

This is a good trick to evaluate the people that you interact with in a professional environment. Have the data ready with you, especially of the people you interact with daily. Remember, you do have different types of needs, which include daily, weekly, monthly, annually, and one-time special needs. Your daily interactions will be easy if you know who has similar thoughts. At times you want to share your thoughts with people who have a different personality than yours (D-type) and at times you only want to share your thoughts with people who have a similar personality (S-type). When would you use this technique? The first one, (D-type), should be used when you know that you have to deal with people with the power play influence. If you bounce your ideas and thoughts off people who have a different personality then there is a fair chance any loopholes would be easily identified. The second option (S-type) should be tried when you have a thought and want to make sure that almost everyone has a pre buy-in with your idea or thought.

Let us understand this by using examples: Have you observed that you connect very fast with some people that you just started interacting with? Your ideas are similar, your approach to problems is similar. Has that happened with you? This is also referred to as having common ideology.

Ideology* can be further classified as:

- Anarchism
- Conversation
- Environmentalism
- Gender Equality
- Liberalism
- Nationalism
- Religious Ideologies
- Socialism

The belief system in these ideologies also aligns when it comes to understanding the type of the individuals you would be negotiating with. Some individuals have a strong belief in these ideologies and some just don't.

The personality of the individual is influenced by the ideology they believe in as well.

When your discussion with an individual clicks and you feel very comfortable talking to that individual you could start to understand that there are many ideologies that you agree on as far as thought process is concerned or that your broad categories explained in chapter 9 are aligned.

If you have almost everyone agreeing to your thought before the actual decision, the support system and your chance to win automatically improves. Remember, it's not the actual negotiation that is critical; it's always understanding the agenda which is crucial and which increases the chances of winning and achieving the need.

* Source: https://en.wikipedia.org/wiki/List_of_political_ideologies

Key Learnings

---

1. You have a good chance of winning if you are not negotiating with a person of similar thought.

2. Understanding the agenda is crucial.

Chapter 18

I Am Shy

I get to meet a lot of people, given the number of years that I have been in the corporate world. When I talk to them about negotiations or even just about understanding the agenda, I often get to hear that "I am shy" or "I feel nervous" or "People don't listen to my opinions". My first comment to them is its ok. It is normal to be nervous. At times it's not even nervousness, it's a fear we have about the repercussions of the negotiation as we have not focused on understanding the agenda. How do we handle such scenarios, where people are more afraid than shy to negotiate? In general, if you are shy as an individual this would be a good time for you to open up. A message for you explicitly here is: "What do you have to lose?" There is a chapter in this book which talks about "What is the worst thing that can happen?" Exactly my point here! If you continue to remain shy in everything you do, you can lose out on opportunities. So, what is critical in such a situation? No matter how shy you are or how weak you feel when it comes to communication, you should practise "getting your point across" or "delivering your message clearly". Say it in fewer words; say it only once... but say it! If you normally don't talk much or fall in the category of "shy" or "nervous" when it comes to negotiating, Stop!!! Think hard!!! Articulate in your mind that "one sentence" which will get your message across to the target audience **in the manner they would understand.** Guess what!! After you make that statement you are done and you can go back to your shyness—your point is communicated well and you are done for the day. So what is this "in the manner they would understand?" This depends on how well you know your audience. If you don't understand your audience well and you speak for hours it is not going to help and you will not be in a condition to connect. While I feel this is an important topic, I also feel this is one place where a lot of individuals need help. While delivering the few lines that you are going to say, the human connection plays an extremely important role here.

I am sure almost everyone who is reading this book would have understood the term "ice-breaker". If there is silence in the room or you are new to a table this would be one line that you would deliver to get people's attention or break the silence in the room. Like ice-breaker, for my shy friends I would like to introduce the term "ssup". Wait! This is already used in many countries as a greeting so what new concept am I introducing here? Shy people that are forced to talk use particular words almost every time they start their sentence. Some people have a habit of starting their discussion with "well", some people start with "you know". Some use the word "actually", some use "hey", while there are some who use "hmmm". There are many other words that I have heard people start their sentence with or use within their sentence multiple times. I like to call them the "ssup" comments.

You are who you are and no matter how hard anyone tries to change you, you remain what you want to be. Using the "ssup" comments in every sentence or in-between your sentence is not good, but if that helps you overcome your shyness then so be it. The only thing I would like you to watch out for is to know your "ssup" comment. While you are trying to deliver your message, keep track of the "ssup" comments and make sure you try to reduce their usage as you improve on your capability to negotiate.

We had a professor in our school whose "ssup" comment was "you know". We, as students in his class, counted the number of times he would use "you know". The irony here was instead of us focusing on the subject he was teaching we kept counting the "you know". After the class we would then compare our numbers. His "ssup" comment would vary from 40 to 50 per lecture of 45 minutes to sometimes going to more than 200 times. In a 45 minutes (equating to 2700 seconds) lecture if you uses the "ssup" comment more than 200 times imagine the plight of the people who have to listen to you. Kids were not interested in learning from the professor as he could not keep them engaged in the learning. Was he shy? Or did he have a challenge articulating his thought? Now that I look back at the interactions we had with him, he would fall in the category of "I am shy". His shyness and/or nervousness were covered with "you know". He had a chance to make a mark on his students; the only mark he left was negative.

I have met people in life at very senior positions in the corporate world, for whom presenting their thought at a leadership discussion or with a large audience is part of their daily job. They still feel very comfortable talking on a personal level especially in a 1-on-1 setting. However, for them to come out in the open and talk to an audience required extreme efforts from their side to break the "I am shy" mode.

Just knowing who you are helps you build the techniques you need to deal with the state you are in. It's ok if you are one of those folks that do not feel comfortable with a large audience. What would be bad is, when you are in front of a mass or a larger audience, not knowing that your facial expression and speech make it clear that you are not comfortable in the current state and you are ready to give anything to get out of that situation. We are talking negotiation folks, and if that is your weakness then those who want to win with you will put you in such a state that you would cave in to all their needs. So, besides ice-breakers, what are your options here? Being prepared, and very well prepared, helps. You get in, make your speech, get your point out and be out of that discussion. Have others chime in for you. Make it interactive, ask questions to the audience. These would be questions that you would have thought in advance for the occasion. Getting through just an hour of discussion to get your one need across is not really a big deal, if you are prepared for the situation.

Key Learnings

1. *If you remain shy you can lose out on opportunities.*
2. *Ice-breakers and good preparation help to overcome difficult situations.*

Chapter 19

Is That Supposed to be Funny?

What would happen if you are not taken seriously in a particular situation or discussion? This is the moment of pulling in the "Is that supposed to be funny?" look. Giving the serious look and a serious message is quite critical to making sure that the level set is confirmed. Body language plays a big role here. I am not asking you to frown. The word frown has at times given a wrong connotation to the message and it can backfire. I have also tried the cross hands posture (crossed at chest) which says I am putting a barrier between me and the person I am talking to. What has really worked for me is "serious smile". Note, it's not "serious laugh".

Giving a serious look can sometimes be tricky. If you are in a sitting posture, putting your hand on your cheek and bending forward as if you are really paying attention, gives a serious look. Keep your eye on the subject but do not cross your legs. If you are in a standing position and have a chair in front of you, hold it with firm straight hands and bend forward slightly. Since your hands are straight, your body should come forward. Your eyes should be on the subject. With a smile on your face, asking the tough question or responding in a tough manner is what I am talking about.

Your intention is not to scare the subject but to make sure the subject understands the serious mode you are in, and the seriousness of the situation or the discussion.

While the "Is that supposed to be funny" look helps you appear serious, make sure that it does not make you look like a snob in a bad mood. There is a thin line between the two; at times people might misunderstand your intention or think that you do not understand. Reiterating the understanding also helps to make sure you are on the same page on the theory that is being explained to you. Reiterating means "explaining the situation back to the person in your own words" to ensure that they understand. In the corporate world we say, "Let me rephrase what you just said, to ensure we are on the same page".

This is an interesting look and getting it right will really be fun. This look can tire the other person out. After the "Is that supposed to be funny" look, to break the tension during negotiations, I have had to joke so that the individual does not get scared or lose the interest to negotiate.

I have seen many people who are not comfortable with confrontational discussions. Whilst the confrontational discussions are supposed to be serious and have to be precise with correct constructive feedback, it's critical that we really do not also put on a very serious face, which might then turn it into a threatening more than confrontational meeting. It is always advised that a confrontational meeting be held in a one-on-one setup. Trying to provide a confrontational message with the "Is that supposed to be funny" look in an open space or forum is psychologically treated as a threat.

So ensure that you are in a private setting or in a closed room with just the two of you, one person providing the confrontational feedback and the other one receiving it.

A recommendation for this meeting: Keep your ears open and "listen" to the discussion as well. Don't just call the person for the confrontational meeting, give the person "Is that supposed to be funny look", make your point, and leave. That entire setting is a bad idea.

This look really enhances the "listening" skills as well, so practise it well. If you are sitting and have your hand on your chin or cheek, bend forward as if you are really paying attention. Don't cross your legs but keep your eye on the subject with a smile on your face as if you are trying to tell the person "I know".

The idea is to ensure that the person you are having the confrontational message with gets a clear message and signal that you are serious but in the environment you are in this is not a threat of any sort. This look can be an easy alternative to that and would help with discussions which might need confrontation.

The virtual "Is that supposed to be funny" is also a trick especially if a lot of your transactions are on the phone like mine. In the corporate world, a lot of discussions and negotiations happen on conference calls. Deals are signed, projects are assigned, topics negotiated, goals are aligned, practically every activity related to work that can be done in person is done over the phone. Getting the message on the phone is tricky but not impossible. Most of the time we have to judge the expressions of the person, the thoughts of the person, the agenda of the person by the tone modulations on the phone. When there is either a confrontational meeting or there is a need for "Is that supposed to be funny" message passed on the phone, I make a sound which sounds, on the phone, like a smile but a bit reluctant at the end. Just a small laugh sound would do the magic as well. You just want to ensure that the person at the other end of the phone line gets a message that there was a "break" of some sort applied.

Recently, at a restaurant, we ordered a few items and somehow the order was messed up. We were talking to the manager on the issue, when a gentleman interrupted us, indicating that we came to this restaurant by our choice and hence did not have a right to complain or make recommendations. Oh!! This was a perfect "Is that supposed to be funny?" moment. I was standing politely but had to get my message across subtly. **A "Smile" drives people crazy, if you get that smile right!! It**

would be very difficult to understand if it is a laugh, a smirk or an insane moment.

If you plan to pick this trick up, use the mirror to see how you look.

Key Learnings

1. *Use this look when you are not taken seriously in a situation.*
2. *The intention should be to get the message across that you are serious.*

Chapter 20

Third Play

"Third Play" is an interesting idea, and in today's world you can easily see this being used on you all the time. I also like to call it "lack of authority" play. You get into some sort of negotiation and the person comes back with: "Wait please, I need to check with my superiors to close the loop." The way I read it is you are reaching their limited authority (or they want you to feel that you have belled the cat very well), the ball is still in their court but when they bring in the Third Play you will get the feeling: "Oh man, I negotiated heavily, now he needs to go to his superiors which means I am getting a good deal here." This is very common with traders.

People have now mastered this art and for someone to break into this idea, my recommendation is you need to play the same idea on them. Looks simple, right? Well, it might backfire as well, so when the need is high, the stake is high, the amount involved is high, it is completely safe to play this back. You need to be watching out because what you consider as a high amount might not be high for the opposite party. In either case if the amount seems high all plays are fair. Homework helps to play in options as well. Here's an easy way out in case your homework does not seem enough. Third Play will buy you time but will keep the discussion hot. So how do you play the Third Play to your advantage? Don't pull this at the start of the discussion, let the discussion flow. There are times when you need to let your gut kick in before you take a further step.

I was trying to help a friend buy his car. We did the homework, especially on what to expect. We also had a recent data point handy on the type of negotiation that the dealer would do. What we also had was a perspective on the need. In this case our need was high so we were ok to cave in a bit. However, caving in was in the back pocket not the front. We went in to the dealer and made him understand that we had done our research and we meant serious business only if we could agree on terms. Our need was high, so we had to set the pitch. We started to talk (negotiate in real terms) and voilà! He pulled in his Third Play.

I smiled and made sure he knew that I smiled. I told the individual if he could not negotiate with us and had to check with someone else, I would rather just talk to that someone else, so he should call that someone else there to talk. The Third was called. He came in and explained that the first individual was right and they could not make any changes. That was when we pulled out our Third. We indicated that if they could not work with us, we would go to another vendor who was willing. Now, when you pull in your Third, be prepared to answer a few questions. There was no improvement in the situation, so here is what we did: We went outside his office and pretended to make a call to the other dealer. After a little while my friend started getting impatient and so we went back in. This time the other party knew our strength; that we could walk away. However, they also knew our weak point since we came back: that the need probably was high at our end. Earlier, in our first discussion with the Third we had put in a few weird requirements which gave us information about his need: it was high as well. He had to meet the numbers for the month. Eventually, we made the deal. But since we had their weakness at hand, had it been just me, I would have walked away.

Accessories are expensive but when you are buying the big item they can be thrown in.

There is a management term I have learned, it's called billiards shooter. A lot of us have practised this in the past unknowingly. We have seen this practised regularly at home. You want the kids to hear something but you don't want to tell them directly so you will talk to another adult in the house making sure the kids hear it too. Basically, you pass on the message to someone else, indirectly ensuring that the party it is intended for hears it. The other places I have seen it used is when someone talks loudly on the cell phone boasting about their capabilities in front of a crowd. The message there is: I am a great individual and see, here is the proof.

I see Third Play being a similar act where the intended party gets the message but not directly. The approach is slightly different from carrom shooter, but it falls in the same category.

Third Play can be used in a different category. In corporate life, while we negotiate everyday, if the two parties cannot reach a consensus, a third person, normally a neutral person, is brought into the discussion. Sometimes, if people junior to you get into an argument and can't agree then a Third can act as a mediator. In this case, however, we are not using a Third for negotiating, we are using a Third for helping with the decision, which means your normal mechanisms of negotiation have been exhausted and now someone else is needed to make a decision.

Let me highlight a fourth grader example which will help articulate a different way to look at the Third.

I was attending an event in my kid's school. It was a class event where the entire class was going to do a Show and Tell for two separate subjects and highlight the work they did for that semester. The Show and Tell for the first subject was at 9:00 AM and then there was a break for 30 minutes to prepare for the next subject. The kids were busy doing the last minute touch-ups on the charts they had prepared. Some parents were sitting in the class while the others were chatting outside. All of a sudden I heard loud voices. There were two kids who suddenly started arguing and quarrelling because one of the kids spoiled the chart paper of the other one. The teacher was in the class and stepped in. I was sitting and watching the discussion.

Teacher: 1, 2, 3—thumbs up if you are paying attention. (Apparently this is one of the methods used in the class to ensure that the kids are listening to what is being said.)

Teacher: What is the matter, why are you quarrelling?

Kid 1: She (Kid 2) spoiled my chart paper by writing on it.

Kid 2: No, Teacher, I did not write on the chart paper, I don't know who wrote on her paper but it was not me.

Kid 1: Teacher she is not telling the truth, she wrote on my paper and now I don't want to work with her.

Teacher: 1, 2, 3—thumbs up if you are paying attention.

Both kids stopped and looked up at the teacher.

Teacher: This is a class event; we are trying to do this as a class. This is not about us as individuals, it is about the class. This is an event where we want to show how we work and what we (the class) have done together.

Kid 1: So why would she spoil my chart paper?

Kid 2: I did not spoil the chart paper, Teacher; this is not right.

Teacher: Here is what I want you to do. Please go in that corner, just the two of you, and decide how you are going to work together.

Kid 1: But Teacher, she started it.

Kid 2: No, Teacher, she will continue to blame me.

Teacher: Please go to the corner, you have 3 minutes, come back with a resolution.

Both the kids went to the corner and came back after a minute.

Kid 2: She does not want to work with me teacher, I am ready to work; I told her that I will help her get the chart done again, even when I did not spoil it.

Kid 1: I don't want to work with her, I saw her spoil the chart and now she is trying to be nice.

Teacher: We are missing a critical point here, this is an activity for the entire class. Do you want me to cancel all of the class events going forward? Parents have taken pains to come to the school on a working day and now we will ask them to go back without completing the event. This is not about us as individuals. This is about team work and working together. I don't want to know who started it; the key point here is how we, as a class, are going to be completing the Show and Tell. So please put yourself away right now. Also, I am going to be ensuring that for the rest of the year you both sit together and within your discussions figure out a way to work together. Do you want to take time to figure out how you will be completing the chart in another 15 minutes? Or should we be spending the other 10 minutes getting to a resolution?

All the other kids in the class were by now watching the discussion. There was peer pressure on these two kids as well along with a lot of the parents watching the teacher handle the situation.

The work which the teacher did was phenomenal; I am sure she probably does this daily. After everyone was back on their schedule, I stopped by the teacher and told her she did a fabulous job; plus I told her I wish I could record this event as I can replay this as a part of the corporate lessons.

Sometimes in our negotiations we forget the "need of the hour" and bring in our personal differences into the mix. While I understand that it's not always easy to let go of your ego, we do have to keep our need in our mind. If the need is not to work with the other kid then it makes sense to continue the discussion. But the need was to make the chart look pretty and there were only 15 left minutes to do so. This was a great example of a Third Play. The teacher could act as the Third in the discussion when the two could not reach a conclusion and set the correct context, highlight the need of the moment, and close the discussion.

In real life we get hung up on "mine", "she did it", "I did not like what he/she did", "he/she spoiled it", "I can do it better", "I am always right" moments. What we forget very easily is our "need". Is it even worth discussing everything else in the world besides our "need"?

What are we going to get when we bring these disagreements

to the Third? It is going to help reach the "need". One size does not fit all, so the example I used here might not be anything that you can relate to or the situation that you are in might be completely different. The person you are dealing with might be having a "malicious intent" or might have their "agenda"; which might be to make you look bad. In any case, if you have to deal with them to get your work done, an argument or fight is not going to help. The term is "navigating the system" to get your "need achieved". The inner octopus needs to be ready to deal with such scenarios, where, if it is not your "need", do not indulge in heated unnecessary discussions. A casual discussion is fine, as long as emotions don't get added to it.

The point that I want to highlight is that the Third can either help with negotiation or help with decision. The next chapter "Who's Faking?" will be interesting if you are playing this Third.

There is another Third in this play. This Third is the use of someone's name during a discussion. This is an interesting topic by itself. People try to help influence a discussion just using someone's name. According to the research done, here is what would be a right perspective to this issue. In the corporate world, the name of a person who is at the top of the management chain is being used for discussions and in this case they would become the Third. The sad part of this is that the person whose name is being used does not know that decisions are influenced with the mere use of his name. The management term for this is "delegated authority". In the corporate world you will find a lot of people misusing this delegated authority. If you get hit by someone who is using delegated authority, a good way to handle this would be to circle back with that Third to validate the facts.

At home, this is used generally by the kids: Mom told me to do this. Now, mom is not around so where is dad going to check? Grown up kids like us use this often as well. "Santa said if you are naughty then you will not get a gift." Sounds familiar?

The world is full of Thirds. At every moment you will get

to hear about the Third in one way or the other. The key is to know how to deal with this Third.

Key Learnings

1. *This technique involves bringing in a third person to secure your advantage in the negotiation.*
2. *It is important not to bring in personal differences into Third Play.*

Chapter 21

Who's Faking?

Two folks just had a disagreement and now they need someone to help them close the deal. Since they need a negotiation expert they come to you for advice. What would you do?

Negotiating is not just about one trying to negotiate with the other. At times there is a Third and it becomes even more interesting when you, as the Third, are helping someone negotiate or if you are acting as a mediator between two parties. This is the other side of playing the Third.

This chapter talks about what you should do if you are playing the Third. It is very easy to play the Third when you don't have anything at stake or you are not playing any favourites. Here you look for facts and help make a decision based on what you think is right. You want to look at the facts provided and start the "who's faking" practice. Keep a really open mind. Get your clues and check them for accuracy.

At times you will find that people, when in conflict, often bring in emotions. You need to keep your emotions out. Mixing emotions with decisions dilutes the matter and the core is left out. At times it is ok to say "give me a minute to analyze the data". It is always good to take time to understand the problem. When emotions are high, and I have to play the Third where I have no stake in the game, I often start with "what is the problem statement here". It is always good to start with understanding the problem. At times, being neutral is fun. I have been in situations where I have seen people argue about the implementations or solutions, not so much about the actual problem statement.

Let's talk about the problem statement in detail now. How does a mediator truly help when a discussion gets heated up and emotions are really high? I pause and ask the question, "What is the problem statement?" I have often seen, when I ask this question, that there is silence. In the corporate world we call it "crickets". Crickets in this example relates to the insect of that name. It makes a peculiar sound which can be very clearly heard especially during the night since there is complete silence. This is when reality starts to kick in. Have you been in an endless discussion? I have. While initially it's fun to see people argue on baseless points, in the end it really gets boring, tiring, and repetitive.

There are people who talk and talk, use technical jargon so that no one understands, making them the wisest of all. If you ask them to explain it in simple language they get flustered since a lot of the times even they don't know what they just said. It's funny to see this type of people talk and try to flourish. I call them "flowerish", not flourish which actually means to prosper. They have a habit of painting a rosy picture and making it look simple when they themselves are not clear what the problem statement is in the first place.

When I am playing Third, I try to keep at the back of my mind, the categories of people that we studied earlier and that I need to just rely on facts and make sure my facts are right.

It is important that the Third should not play favourites. The discussion can take a twist when the Third has a soft corner for one of the parties. I think we all know playing favourites changes perspective. In the earlier chapter "Trust Your Instincts" we looked at some of these characteristics.

Key Learnings

1. *If you are playing the Third, keep emotion out and look for the facts.*
2. *It is important to first identify the problem statement.*

Chapter 22

SOL

This is another of my favorite topics. SOL stand for "Shit Out of Luck". This is a scenario which we all land up in on a daily basis. This is the moment when you realize you have no chance. This is not a feeling of helplessness. Helplessness is when you feel victimized and feel you having no options left.

SOL is where you are cornered due to the circumstances or, in a lot of the cases, due to lack of anticipation. You did not anticipate that something like this could happen to you. I guess one can still sit and pray in this scenario!

A Serious traffic Jam (SOL)

First Reason (Slow moving vehicles in the middle of the road)

Figure 15A

Main Reason for the traffic Jam
(Animals can't be blamed here as some is driving them in the middle of the road)

Figure 15B

SOL is the state when you start to realize that if you don't do something now you will lose and probably lose badly. For instance, if I already know that I am on a road with slow moving traffic then I should have kept an extra 30 to 40 minutes for travel. The key here is the realization. A moment of realization where we know something adverse is coming our way or a realization that the discussion is going nowhere and we are spinning in circles because the people that we are expecting to deal with don't want a solution or that their agenda is to prolong the discussion as much as possible.

The solution to SOL is also SOL. SOL in the solution mode means "Start out logically". As the wise say, the answer lies within. Before we start to look for answers let's make sure there is realization. A lot of real world problems come all of a sudden. We don't get time to see them coming, correct? I would say, think again before you answer. Most of the time we don't watch for patterns, or we choose to ignore the patterns.

In our example above, if it is already known that the roads are congested during transit, then the planning at our end needs to be to keep extra time for travel.

Scenarios don't build up in a day, keeping our eyes and ears open always helps. Negotiation sometimes pushes us into a corner and the one thing that should come to our grey matter is that we know our strengths and weakness better than anyone else.

For this discussion we go with an understanding that we know our strengths and weaknesses. We need to watch for patterns every minute to understand the ecosystem. This is the ecosystem around us. We cannot really solve the problem of world hunger in a day, so let's focus on you.

Think for a minute what your ecosystem would be. For a normal individual the ecosystem can comprise many of the following: friends, relatives, work, college, school, family, and your interests. Keeping a watch on patterns with everyone in this ecosystem would be too much for anyone. Moreover, just watching the pattern and not reacting at all is also not a good scenario. So here is what I do. I keep a log of patterns around me. At times it becomes useless data and at time it amounts to something useful.

So where do we keep a log? Some people have great brains and a phenomenal memory so they remember a lot. People like me keep a running tab on the gadget they have. When is the data too old? It depends on the type of patterns. There are a few I keep for years and then there are those whose life is six months. You need to finalize your own pattern and retention period. Basically, what I am asking you to do is to keep your eyes and ears open.

In conclusion, start with SOL and watch your ecosystem for patterns to understand the agenda. This is the data you would need when you actually sit at the negotiating table.

Key Learnings

1. ***Most of the time we miss or ignore patterns of events.***
2. ***Find your own way of maintaining a log of patterns.***

Chapter 23

Opinions Are Free

It is good to ask for opinions on topics, get perspectives from multiple angles and cover the base if you missed out on some interesting fact. Everyone, normally, would have an opinion. At times you will feel inundated with opinions that would not help you much. So as a part of data gathering this technique can be used to see if you missed out on any options or to just get a different perspective.

Since opinions are free, with the number of acquaintances we have in our life, we can really collect significant information.

Sometimes you may not like a perspective or opinion but don't forget to respect others' opinions and perspectives. If you don't like them that's fine, but if someone is taking the pain to express an opinion, respect that. We need to take the necessary time to digest the opinions of others. At times we are in a rush to prove our point thereby losing focus on the actual topic in question. There is a message I want to emphasize; it is called the "Art of asking the right question". If we ask the right questions, opinions can really be valuable and we can use opinions to our advantage. From my perspective, no question is stupid if you frame your question right; it's the answer that we might not agree with. So what is framing the question right? This would get you into the art of asking the right questions. Questions can be open-ended questions, close-ended questions, provocative questions and so on. I always feel a question should be thought-provoking. The type of question would depend on the scenario one is in. If you need to eat food and are hungry, after reaching the restaurant asking open-ended questions can make you perish from hunger. There you would need a close-ended question: "What is the quickest thing available from the menu? Please get it."

Opinions are valuable but if you just rely on opinions you can again deviate from the key that we are trying to talk about here: "Need". Yes, that does not change. The other side of this scenario is that people will give opinions whether you want them to or not. You start a discussion and almost everyone in the discussion will start shooting out opinions. Of course, everyone will give you an opinion to suit their own agenda. We need to be careful about what to keep and what to let go from the opinions. It does not take time for opinions to turn into advice. This should be the signal for you to stop asking for opinions. It is so easy to critique a situation. I am not demeaning the job of the folks who get paid to critique a situation or restaurant or movie. I am talking about people who critique or provide their advice on any and every situation. These are the people you don't want an opinion from. Why? Well, they feel they know everything and it is their birthright to provide advice in any and every situation. While taking an opinion is good, taking unwanted advice is not. So where do we balance the act then? The way I like to deal with this situation is this: If I go to someone with a problem statement, I am looking for an opinion. If someone comes to me with unsolicited advice, I smile and remember this chapter that I wrote.

Key Learnings

1. Opinions should be sought as part of data gathering.

2. Take only the advice that is useful.

Chapter 24

Oh Man, It's KIN!

When negotiating with kin, even if your intentions are good, the emotions are always high. Here I have seen that no one considers whether the need is high or low. All the buzz words like feelings, heart, care, and ego are used, making the discussion challenging. Sometimes, just a mere discussion ends up in a negotiation battle. I am carefully using the word battle and not war, because in this situation we really care or it is perceived that we really care. When the negotiation starts it's never easy—if you make it to an easy one you got lucky here. I feel it would be fair to say one size fits all does not work in this scenario. This is really a sensitive topic and, especially for people that really do not want to hurt others, a very challenging one. So what should one do then? I am sure almost everyone will agree with me that this is one discussion where you will need to keep your brain in the right place. Thinking will be one of your most important data collection techniques. What people might have a struggle with is the implementation of the thought process especially since the emotions are high or, at times, extremely high. I have seen scenarios where most of the techniques listed in this book have to be used at the same time or at known intervals, to deal with one scenario. Here, getting prior consensus, as we learned in the "similar poles repel" chapter also becomes important and very relevant. I have learned that trying to please everyone is seldom going to work; you will end up hurting someone or the other. So the other technique to remember along with the need and the prioritization of the need is whom you could hurt in case push comes to shove. A backup plan needs to be kept handy; we will talk about the backup plan in detail in the last chapter of this book. For now let's go with the assumption that a backup plan is needed. What else can help us when we are dealing with kin? Remember the human connection? The connection would play a great role here.

I remember a situation where there was a huge disconnect between two people in the family. When I decided to "play the Third", one party felt I was supporting the other individual more than him. I was literally yelled at (you know how families behave when stakes are high) and had to get out of the room. I took a 30 minute break and came back. While it gave them time to think about what they did, I was able to cool off as well. We then started again, trying to understand the "need of the hour". At times people carry "baggage" with them, especially when it's kin. A discussion of what happened 10 years ago is brought into play when there is no need or relevance for it. Broken relationships hurt more and so when "push comes to shove" or when you take the final decision, if possible choose a neutral part. Don't cut the relationship, limit the interaction. It's called the "Hi-Hello" relationship. No interaction beyond that. It's tough but better than breaking a relationship; the difficult part is sticking to the "Hi-Hello" only and not getting carried away with emotions.

When possible try to deal in a rational manner in these scenarios. A rational, sane, logical manner would mean where possible try to be fair. I had to use the term "where possible". Remember, life is not fair. Justification for your actions would also be very necessary and relevant in this case. The justification would help understand "Why" you did what you did. Understanding the repercussions or the end result upfront will help. In this case it is critical to keep a tab, as losing relationships normally hurts. Use all the right terms and keep your agenda straight to the point. The more you twist it, the more complicated it gets. The more you pull the idea of reaching a resolution, the more convoluted this one gets. Keep your needs in mind, be "rational" and close the gap as soon as you can. Beyond that, there is only so much one can do.

Key Learnings

1. *Dealing with kin involves emotion and ego.*
2. *Remember to have a rational, unbiased approach to the negotiation.*

Chapter 25

I Always Lose When I Am Angry

This chapter will explain how to deal with the situation when you feel angry. I like to call myself the "Loser Me" when I feel the need to show anger. All of us come across difficult situations. When the mind is not stable, it makes the discussion factor more complicated. We end up losing the "Cool Me" under pressure. We either become defensive or irritated when we see things are not going as planned or expected. Sometimes it's the sheer pressure or stress to deliver which throws us out of control. There are a few human emotions that are very risky to have around us when the stakes are high, namely anger, fear, suspicion, losing faith, or just sheer pressure of defeat. In any discussion, if your mind is not stable or you are losing focus, stop the discussion right there if you can. Your brain is not helping you at that point and you are just reacting by impulse. You are not thinking of options, your brain is not at all rational, you get into the "It's my way" mode and the only thought in your mind is "How can this person tell me such a thing!" All you are trying to do at that minute is prove yourself right and prove the other wrong. It is almost as if the thinking power shuts down, which is really dangerous, especially for you. People enjoy making others angry because it's fun for them and it gives them a chance to win. It would be really nice if all of us could control our feelings in the first place and not get angry.

My six-year-old tells me, "Dad, when I get angry I feel powerful." Do you really feel powerful when angry? There are many faces of anger starting from change in physical metabolism to facial expressions to tone of speech. *Research says your heartbeat increases when you get angry. You tend to breathe faster, your muscles tighten and your body temperature could increase as well. The reality is we are human and everyone has a "moment". When you have the moment, try to stop the negotiation. Getting away, changing the topic, listening patiently, or just taking a five minute break will help. If you cannot stop the discussion, try to take the path which will give you the lowest hit. While angry you are in no state to win since you technically do not have control over your actions. So what is your option here? Lose less. Either you control your emotions or get ready to lose. If a discussion or a topic makes you angry, try to separate the person and the situation. People have a tendency to get carried away. You are not happy with the situation at that time so stop being mad at the person because to be honest that is exactly what people are looking for. As soon as someone is angry he or she becomes a victim. People feel that raising their voice gives the strength and power they want the world to see in them. Getting angry or showing anger is not going to help (unless you are faking anger).

A good friend and an ex-colleague of mine talked about a technique she uses to fake anger. I want to dedicate this technique to her; however, I have changed her name in the book. We will call this technique the "Julia moment". Every Thursday, I and my peer managers at a multinational company in US went out for breakfast. This was a ritual we started

---

*Source: Anger Research Consortium; American Psychological Association

because we would not get enough time during office hours to catch up on what was happening in our world or teams. This ritual brought all of us in a comfort zone and since there was no threat amongst us due to the unique roles we played, our discussions were amiable and helpful to each other. On one of those Thursdays, she came a little late to the breakfast, smiled at all of us and sat down. Her smile indicated that she had done something unusual and was proud of the way she had handled the situation. Upon probing, she started talking about the incident. She had two grown up boys, I should say three if we include her husband in the list. The previous day when she went home, her house seemed to be in a mess with every object all over the place. If you have three boys in the house what else can be expected? After entering her home, she started picking up things as she was entering through the living area. In her words, "I yelled at everyone in the family, I showed my blaaaaaaaah moment, I called everyone by their first names as I stood in the middle of the living room" as all three of them came running to the living room. "I showed them what 'lost it' looks like. I showed them how mad I could get. Two hours later the whole house looked like home, the way I like to look at". She then softly put her hands on the table as she smiled and drank the black coffee she had ordered. All of us at the table looked at each other, picked up our coffee mugs and said "Cheers". She was a very soft spoken individual and her use of this technique to highlight, faking anger, is an art. If done correctly it can produce miracles. If, however, you get carried away while faking the anger, a lot could go wrong.

Faking anger is a technique and you can use it to your advantage. Assume you are faking anger—the person on the other side may think this is a good time for him as you have lost it now. I have started to believe that instead of getting angry it's good to fake anger and not lose yourself in the first place. If you start to digress from the reality, get your brain thinking "loser" and try to regain yourself as soon as you can. Or else just end the discussion or negotiation. It's ok to say you am not in the mood to argue at that time. Is arguing the same as being angry? I don't believe so. When you argue, you are making a point or expressing your opinion. Argument, if used diligently, can help with conflict management. Arguing is ok, settling disputes equitably is ok, as long as emotions are not high. Healthy argument is valuable and should always be welcomed, as long as it stays healthy.

The message I have for folks here is that when you have your "moment" and it is possible to stop the discussion, please do stop the discussion and move on to something else. If you have tried all options and have no other possibility but to continue the discussion, take a break for 10 to 15 minutes or a little longer if possible and come back to the discussion. I have, when it is possible, joked and said, "Guys, I am having the moment, can we please do this discussion some other time?" The main point is, when possible walk away or stop the discussion; if no other options are available then delay the discussion and get a hold over your emotions. My kids and I play this game. When they get angry with me I get to show them the loser signal and when dad has his moment the kids are free to show me the signal. This really helps us realize that the situation is not healthy and something needs to change within that environment.

There is a technique called "Go blank" which can be used when you feel the urge to show your anger to the world. If you are "faking anger" you are good, but if you are really angry, don't utter a word—not a single word,—don't agree on anything, don't disagree on anything, close yourself within yourself and feel like you just went "blank". No reaction, no questions, just listen, or even shut yourself further and don't even listen. The only thing you are working on at that moment is trying to get a grip on yourself. See the image of a loser in your mind's eye and remain blank till you feel you can handle it. One can additionally use the technique of "Is that supposed to be funny?" that we learned earlier. A person who can defuse a high-tension situation would be a hands-on specialist who has mastered the **"Art of understanding the Loser Me"**.

Figure 16

Key Learnings

---

1. *When you are angry your reactions can be unstable and irrational.*
2. *When angry, walk away, or stop or delay the discussion.*
3. *Faking anger in a situation is better than really getting angry.*

Chapter 26

The Real Fun ...

Understanding the agenda of multiple entities or parties within a negotiation has its own fun. This is where you need to draw up a chart of the people you are dealing with. You will need to do a lot more research before you get started and might run into a time crunch if you take a lot of time to analyze.

There are different types of players you deal with in a negotiation. Some get along well with you; some get along well amongst themselves. Some of the people might have known each other for a while; there are a few outliers. It's a "combination mystery" one has to deal with. Some are very well connected socially while there also might be some with silo mentality. The technique I am going to talk about takes 3 to 4 hours of serious thinking to put the puzzle together.

Start with identifying all the stakeholders in the discussion. Now put their names on a piece of paper and connect them with relationships amongst them. Connect the individuals as shown in the example below. The thickness of the line indicates the type of bonding. A thick line as in the case of Persons 3 and 4 indicates a strong bonding. In the example below if Person 1 has key negotiations to be done with Person 2, the only way to approach Person 2 is through the established connection of Person 1 ←---→ Person 4 ←---→ Person 5 ←---→ Person 2.

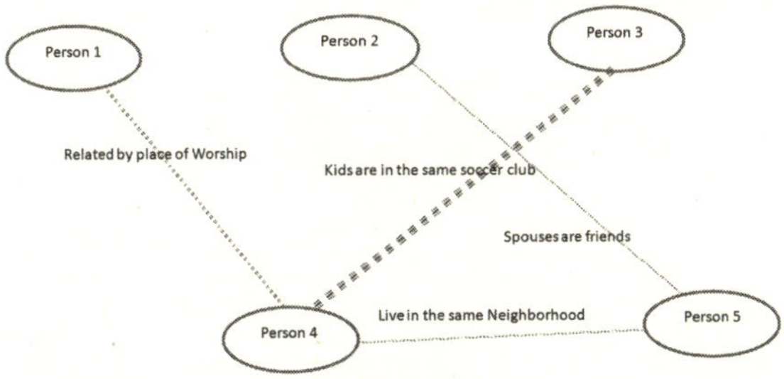

Figure 17

Now, in the next example, how do you think Person 1 will connect with Person 2?

Person 1 ←---→ Person 4 ←---→ Person 3 ←---→ Person 2

Obviously through the lines that have thick connections, right? But why? The connections that were explored in the previous example still exist so why was there a need to change the tactic? What you need to watch for is how best you can move the needle. If you do enough research and establish upfront connections, then your approach would be in the right direction.

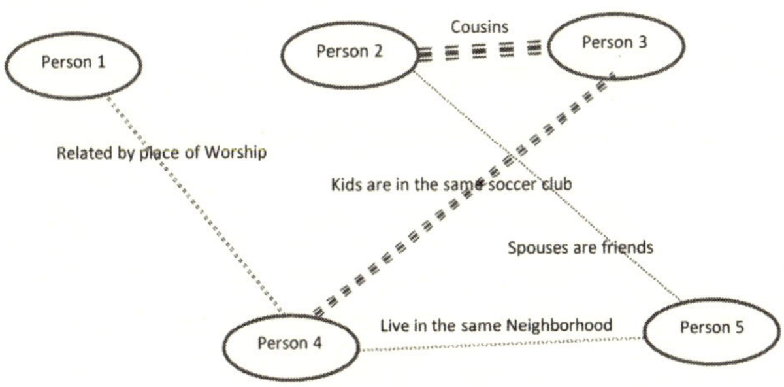

Figure 18

The real fun section cannot be completed until one talks about the "micro-message" these people would share amongst themselves. That has to be a trigger for you to complete your story and if you have this data then it would be worth spending the 3-4 hours we talked about. It would definitely help you move the needle very fast.

Key Learnings

1. *It is important to understand the agenda of the multiple parties in a negotiation.*
2. *Note down the connections between all the stakeholders for your research.*

Chapter 27

Give More, Take Everything

So you are almost at the end of the book. What have you picked up so far? Think of one thing—just one thing—that this book has helped you with. If reading this far you have still not found that one thing, let's see if this chapter helps. The technique that this chapter deals with is called "Give more take everything".

"Give more take everything" sounds contradictory. Well, that is the approach that needs to be taken in this technique of negotiation. People should feel they are in charge when negotiating with you while the fact is that you are giving more to the person to take everything you "need" away. Going back to basics, the need that you have should be met else the negotiation is not successful. When you get into negotiation, making the first move helps but not making the first move also helps. Confusing? Yes. How can making the first move help, while not making the first move help as well?

The statement is contradictory: should we make the first move or not?

Let me first talk about the advantages of making the first move. You can agree upfront on the things you care about the most, this is to your advantage. What did you do here? You gave your agenda away, which also means that you gave away your need so the other side knows your weakness. At times this is okay—eventually you want to close the deal. When the need is high your inclination here is to let go of anything else but your core. On the flip side it gives the other person an indication of your need. When making the first move, especially during negotiation one can start to talk about non-trivial topics so that the individual you are dealing with will think that those non-trivial topics are what is important to you. As they prepare to respond to those non-trivial scenarios, you add more to that by saying "Oh, by the way..." which is what your actual need is. This is also called "false distraction".

So how will not making the first move help as well? By not making the first move and allowing the other person to make his move, you can get an idea of the need of the other person and then deal with things around it. When we started the book we talked about keeping the end in mind. Your end needs to be clear at least in your own mind. If it means you have to give a lot to get what you eventually need, it is still a win from your perspective. After all, you got what you needed. Well, this can be debated. If you lose everything else but get what you want that is not a true win.

Think about it: you started the discussion for a cause. A few things were on the agenda and you wanted to get that straight. A good example here is "salary discussion". The first one who makes a move in the figure sets the "bar". If the human resource specialist you are dealing with tells you a number, you respond "under influence" of that number with a number which is just a few notches away from that, planning to get a little more than what they quoted. Instead if salary was the "need" you were looking for, giving that upfront might help alleviate the pain at a later state. There are techniques to negotiate on salary and we are not covering those here as I have seen people recommend that you should never give out what you are looking for in the first go. Always let the human resource specialist come out with their number first, they "might" give you a lot more than what you had in mind. Obviously that can backfire as well, as they might make a very low quote and all your energy might be spent on just bringing that number up. It all depends on your "need". You want to use the technique which fits your "need" the most.

Key Learnings

1. Making the first move can help but not making the first move can also help.

2. Understand how both can benefit you in the context of your need.

Chapter 28

The Easy Sell

This is a tricky one. Have you seen a deal which looked very easy and you thought you did a great job at that one? Well, think why it would be so easy. Most likely it was predetermined with enough margins in-between to make it look easy. Remember any such incident? In an earlier chapter "Connecting the Dots" we mentioned "the Easy Sell syndrome", so let us understand what the easy sell syndrome is: A deal that is going exactly your way without any effort from you. The thought that should come to mind is, "This looks too good to be true".

I have seen many examples and incidents of this type. Obviously not all Easy Sell syndromes would fall in this category but most of them do. Others' dire "needs" might become your advantage in this case and would fall in the Easy Sell syndrome but in most cases when you see an easy sell start thinking of the hidden agendas here. Remember, "everyone has an agenda". See if you can get to the other person's agenda, and why they are making it easy for you. Sometimes you find people helping you for no gain of theirs, creating paths for your negotiation and win....do you think it is that easy? The initial 5 minutes explained earlier comes very handy if we do our job right. "There is a reason for everything", sometimes you see it clearly and at times you have no idea what just happened. You might fall prey to a well-calculated agenda that someone had planned. In the past I have struggled with the Easy Sell. I could sense someone is making an Easy Sell and I could see the agenda behind it as well, but I would still want to fall for it knowing very well what I was getting into.

The situation I just described is sometimes a good situation to be in. In the end you are getting what you signed up for. If you know what you are getting into it's a good thing, right? It is, in fact, scary. You think you know… but you are not sure if you know…. which is "half knowledge" and that is dangerous. When you sense that Easy Sell cards are put on the table my recommendation is just finish the game right there. Make sure the people or teams you are negotiating with understand that you know their game but are still playing it as you don't want to beat around the bush. It's out in the open; you know an Easy Sell is pulled on you. The person you are dealing with also knows that you understand they are pulling the Easy Sell. There is a look I use during the Easy Sell: the "Do you think I was born yesterday?" look. It's a smirk with eyebrows raised, as if you are surprised that they tried to pull the Easy Sell on you. Make it clear that you know the drill very well. That would change the perspective of the person you are dealing with. Now that the cards are on the table and both of you are clear that the game is still played because the "needs" of both are met, you are going along with the Easy Sell—not because you don't like to win, but just because your "needs" are being met. You don't have all the time in the world and you have other priorities too. After all, you have your agenda too!

Key Learnings

1. A deal going your way without any effort is usually too good to be true.

2. It's ok to fall for the easy sell, if "needs" are met.

Chapter 29

Let It Go—It's Over

It is a tough call to "let it go". It is difficult for us to "really let it go" in respect of anything. We hold on to a lot of memories, unwanted things, unrealistic demands, grudges, and unnecessary wishes. Have you heard the phrase "Dude! It's over, let it go"? If not, its time you hear it from me. Someone needs to make folks realize there are times when you have to tell yourself "let it go—it's over". The reason this is an important message to know is because until we have the ability to realize when to let it go we will hold on to it. If you continue to pursue beyond a point, you are going downhill from there. People will lose interest even in talking to you, forget dealing with you. So when would it be a moment for one to realize it's over? Remember some things which we talked about in our earlier chapters. Need has to be high, data has to be solid, multiple tricks can be tried in one go. I have seen that when the need is low it is easy to let go. However, with higher needs it becomes challenging. I have talked to many individuals on this topic and almost everyone struggled with this one. We stick to our ideas, thoughts, beliefs, and sometimes it's plain ego. I remember once we were in a small town on a trip to the Rockies, USA, and were craving for good food. I very well remember we paid three times the price we would pay in a normal restaurant to satisfy our need! My friend who accompanied us on the trip commented that "at this price we can feed a family of 12". We knew the price we were paying was high but so was the need to eat good food. In those days the GPS did not exist, hence our data collection was bad and our need was high so technically we just "let it go". We had one more choice and clearly we did not execute that choice. The choice was to let go of the need. In reality there are multiple choices at hand every time but at times we put blinders on and just focus on the need. This can burn us if we do not "let the wrong need go". I call this craving. Technically there is no right or wrong need; it's all in the perspective. I will use my comment that I used in the previous chapters again: "It's all a matter of mind, if you don't mind it does not matter". So who determines if the need is right or wrong? It's you, and only you. We have chances to make mistakes when the need is high and if we continue to stick to it even when we know this we will not get it. At times it has daunted me as well in negotiations that while I am careful not to hurt feelings or not focus on the individual and just focus on the situation at hand, the people that I am dealing with don't look at the scenario in a similar fashion. Hence the comment **"It's good to let it go sometimes not because you don't care, but because they don't."** No regret then becomes a critical part of this chapter. People have a great tendency of continue to remember what they let go. Having regrets about what you have let go is not going to help you. The more you think about it the more it will bother you. In this chapter when I say "let it go", I mean let everything go, the idea, the thought, everything, and do not bring in regrets as well.

Key Learnings

---

1. Sometimes it is best to let go of things.

2. Never have regrets about having let go of something.

Chapter 30

Walk Away

Negotiation, and Walking away? Aren't these two contradictory? Let's explore this further.

I feel walking away, if done right, is an art. While it gives an impression to the other person that you are not interested or you simply don't care about what you are negotiating, it also gives you an option to see how curious or desperate the other person is. When you either walk away or start to walk away, sometimes you see the true colours of the other person. If the other person is desperate or getting close to being desperate, they will cave in more than you expect. When you are well into a discussion and all of a sudden you stop showing interest or use the "walk away" syndrome, you will add a few benefits to your negotiating power. I would like to highlight here that this is a known secret and people have played this in the past, sometimes knowingly, sometimes unknowingly.

Walking away does not mean insulting and walking away. It just means that you are not interested in that discussion or deal at that moment since you feel this will be endless and would not spin the way you want it to spin. Eventually, you have to consider why you are negotiating in the first place:

to get something out of the negotiation, correct? If there is no win whatsoever and you have to accept all the terms of the individual you are negotiating with, what is the point? Thinking of this from the agenda perspective, there is enough time spent on a discussion, both from your standpoint and from that of the person you are negotiating with. Both have invested energy into a discussion which shows signs of getting somewhere. Then you decide to walk away instead. Did the person lose everything? What about your time? Sure, you also spent time on the discussion but you decided to walk away with a hope that the other person would call you back at that moment or later since they have a bigger need. If it's a product then you surely have an edge. Walking away helps getting the ambiguity clarified. You took your stand by clearly indicating that your need is not high here. Technically what you also indicated by "walking away" is that you don't care; the ball is now in the other person's court. It puts solid pressure on the other person if the need on the other side is high. But you would not have known that if you would not have walked away. Correct?

Walking away also helps to clarify your "intention" here. If I was on the other side of someone "walking away" on me, I would interpret it as "either this individual is desperate to get it" or he "really does not need it". So I would not take a walk away lightly. Here is where I would look at body language. The body language would tell me a lot about that individual, if I need to follow-up on the walk away with some kind of technique or "let it go". Walk away is a very powerful tool, if used correctly, especially if we clearly understand the agenda of the person. This could be a suicidal move for you if the need is high at your end. I would recommend not walking away when you are working on understanding someone's agenda in the first place or if you are dealing with someone who is your kin. Walk away also can be used when you really understand the Agenda and know that the "need" of the person you are dealing with is "higher" than your "need". In that case this will be one of the best techniques to use.

Key Learnings

1. Walking away indicates that you are not interested in the deal at that point.

2. Never have regrets about having let go of something.

Chapter 31

What's Your Backup Plan?

Now that we have covered a lot of aspects of negotiation, the last but not the least key around negotiation is having a backup plan.

If you start a discussion, and, with the tips listed earlier, find out early in the game that this is not an easy one and you will not get the exact need that you have in mind, then having a backup plan helps. I also like to call it "what have you got to give" or in other terms, what can you let go, to reach closer to your need. It is always easy to fall back, if you have a backup plan. Your backup plan is "your" backup plan so you cannot disclose it. However, you need one for sure. Why? As explained throughout this book your need has to be clear in your mind—what you can let go to achieve your need is equally important. The higher the "needs", the stronger the backup plan should be. You might have to give away everything just to achieve the key need you have. A good backup plan makes your negotiation easy. At times I end up revealing a fake backup plan just to get the attention of the other side and make them believe that they are now getting ready to win. Making them look like a winner could very well be your backup plan. Note: we are only trying to satisfy our "need"; anything more than that is technically "additional baggage" that you might have to carry. So always focus only on the "need" and your backup plan should be aligned to "save your need".

Plan your session: write down what you are going to achieve, keep it in your back pocket and if you need to pull it out during the negotiation—it's ok!! It just shows that you are prepared. It goes without saying that if your backup plan is well-articulated in your mind, you will do much better during the discussion since you would have thought about multiple scenarios already. The better prepared you are, the better you will do not just in negotiation but overall in life as well. So taking it a step further, always have a backup plan because "everyone has an agenda" and now we know how to handle that!

Key Learnings

1. *Having a backup plan is important during negotiations.*
2. *The more prepared you are, the more you are likely to succeed.*

Chapter 32

What Is the Worst Thing That Can Happen?

I thought of keeping this as the last chapter in the book. We talked about this topic a little earlier in a different context where I emphasized that there is no harm trying or asking for more. You did not have anything in the first place and you will be getting into negotiation to get some need satisfied. Now that you have started negotiating, obviously the need is high, so it is ok to ask. And it is ok to ask for more, why not? I have asked myself this question many times before starting a negotiation. The people that know me well have heard this from me multiple times in several scenarios. I have this question always answered before I take on the negotiation. "What is the worst thing that can happen?" or "What could be the worst case scenario of the negotiation I am going to have?" Obviously when it comes to work or if I have to negotiate during the tenure of the role I am playing in a corporate, a lot of the times the answer to this question is easy. "I might lose my job!" Don't get me wrong. I am not trying to scare anyone here but there are very few places or very few people that I have seen who take criticism positively. I am not suggesting that you do not criticize, all I am saying is think of the repercussions. At times we take our decisions based on "zero-risk game". We don't take up a particular scenario, or discuss a particular problem because we don't want to take a risk in that scenario. Ever seen a cat drinking milk? Closing the eyes does not mean no one is looking. It is like an ostrich burying its head in the ground. The thought which they have in mind is, if I don't look at the world, no one will look at me. If your message is not clear, the negotiation might backfire. Even if you explained your problem statement clearly, your feedback might not be taken in the right spirit, since you did not articulate it well.

The power remains in crucial thinking, crucial planning, crucial speech, and crucial message delivery. If the problem is identified and your message is clear, people do take it in the right spirit. At times we get so bogged down trying to explain issues to individuals that we don't focus on the problem statement. There is a way to deliver a message; the key is to master the art of delivering the message. So when we think about what is the worst thing that can happen, also keep in mind what can go wrong if we don't deliver the message correctly. As we continue our effort to learn, there might be a scenario when there might not be a solution. Not everything in the world has a solution, or at least that is what people perceive. I try to put things into perspective and try to put on my rational hat. Putting a rational hat on might not be the agenda of some people who are involved with you in a particular situation. I wish we could make every individual mature enough to think in a rational manner and not have a different "need".

From my perspective "what is the worst thing that can happen" is very important. People, when motivated, try out things without keeping the reality in mind. We live in a real world and that fact will not change. While we try our best to get the right data, get the agenda, do the right negotiation, and give it enough time, we might end up in "Let it go" mode and maybe that is your backup plan, or maybe you want to continue with other techniques if the need remains high.

Remember, one solution does not fit all, and not everything has a solution. Be mature; the definition of mature is "having a fully grown or developed body; grown to full size or having reached a desired state or showing the mental and emotional qualities of an adult." Nowhere in this definition is it said that the person who has the qualities of an adult also needs to react in a rational manner. So the point is, no matter what age you are, have the maturity to think in a rational manner and have the discussion in an adult manner! While almost everyone claims that they are acting maturely, there will be folks that don't get it; if that individual falls within your range of "need" help the person think in a rational manner, else "let it go". We have needs to satisfy.

Key Learnings

1. *Keep in mind that if things do not go as planned there will be repercussions.*
2. *Be real; try to rationally think of the worst that can happen .*

About Indus Source Books

Indus Source Books is a niche, independent book publisher in Mumbai passionately committed to publishing good and relevant literature. We believe that books are one of the most important mediums of communication and we seek to bring out publications that help to serve the community and the world we live in.

At Indus Source Books, we celebrate the diverse spiritual traditions, culture, and history of the world and present it to our readers in a contemporary format that retains its essential flavour: "Indian Spirit, Universal Wisdom".

Visit our website www.indussource.com for more details.

Indus Source Books
PO Box 6194
Malabar Hill PO
Mumbai 400006
India
www.indussource.com
info@indussource.com